COPYRIGHT

First published 2017 by Shaecc Ltd
Bedfordshire

ISBN 978-0-9957980-9-0

Printed in the United Kingdom

SUNNY DAYS

∞

Some days the sun shines at just the right angle for it to reach your soul. You know the times. Nothing can take your joy away. You are (almost) literally walking on sunshine.

Those are sunny days.

Sunny Days is all about perspectives and the way we look at things. It challenges you to consider how you approach life and to work out how to be better at maintaining your personal sunny days.

Sunny Days is filled with reflections from my journey through dark places to sun-filled moments. This book illustrates how we can learn from difficult situations and confirms the notion that trials can serve to make us pure gold. My hope is that each reader will engage in a journey to discover or rediscover their own potential, strength and inner beauty through self-reflection and analysis of the situations that life throws their way.

The Dream Days Collection will improve your position if you allow it to. You just have to engage.

DEDICATION

∞

On June 15th, I was sat in a hotel room playing around with a creative app on my iPad. I wrote a few lines, deleted them. Drew a few images, deleted them. Came up with a few concepts, kept them. Those concepts were the first outlines of the Dreams Days Experience. 365 days later, the first of those books has become a reality.

That year left an impression on me that will be hard to shake. The London attacks, some personal trials and the incident, where a seemingly preventable inferno displaced the lives and loves of so many, left me feeling raw. I consumed the media coverage in tiny, bite-sized portions, afraid that, should I be challenged to withstand the full extent of what had happened, I may never be able to pull myself away.

I was touched by the goodness of others and stories of communities emerging from the thick plumes. Even as I watched, I understood that there were those who still did not know what had become of their loved ones. I was reminded that tears, prayers and pain were bestowed upon us for such a time as this and that without them, we may never find the courage to act, impact and reach out.

My birthdays mean so much more because of all we've been through these last few years. Whether together or apart, one thing that remains true is, as a species, we know how to love. Regardless of how utterly horrid today is, the sun will shine again. We can't break sunshine's cycle. We can depend on it.

I hope this book will help you to face your personal struggles with as much hope and courage as writing it has for me.

CONTRIBUTORS

∞

Thanks for being a rock for me. For the whole time you knew me, I was lost and had no idea who I was. You stayed anyway. When I consider who I am now and the experiences that got me to this point, I have to acknowledge the great ocean of people who helped to forge my path. Some did so positively, some more negatively, but all made an impact! I learned some hard life lessons!

I hope you know what a positive impression your friendship has left on my life and on the choices I've made. There were rubbish times, sure, but our good times outweighed the bad, so to honour that, I will keep the memories of our friendship safe until we have the chance to build new ones.

Honourable Mentions
Keira Allen-Anderson, Ian Reid, Davina Hanson, Charlene Edwards, Donna Hanson, Courtenay Eccleston, Roselyn Stewart, Careen Hanson, Ione Hanson.

Platinum Producers
Juliet Viveen Hanson
This book would not be a reality without your belief in me. Thank you x
Louise Gunter
Thanks for the support and faith. You're the best x

Golden Producers
Andrew McKinley
You have always been supportive and are a true inspiration. Thank you x
Cheryl Ryan
I pray that you gain all the blessings you deserve. You are truly amazing! Thank you x
Alisha Gardiner
I love you like family. Thanks for the memories and support. You're awesome x

Golden Contributors
Johanna Joseph-Croucher
Gabrielle Gittens
Charlene Clarke
Lynda Sears
Nyamboki

Sunny Contributors
Sandra Gunter
Safiya Clunis

Dazzling Contributors
Eisha Hanson
Julette Malcolm
Theresa Davis
Sam Davies
Angela Dube
Siobhan Maragh
Morvette Cummings
Yvonne Reid

Special thanks to:
the nurses on Ward 20, Louise Bolton, Amanda and Carol (the Head and Neck Cancer Liaison Nurses), Jenard Dyer, Clair Lawrence, Gail Windrass, Peter Bailey, Sandy Officer, Cathy Boldeau, Donette Hanson-O'Connor and many others.

SECTION OUTLINE

∞

Each chapter has been divided into seven sections. Those sections have been designed to help you get the most out of The Dream Days series of books.

You do not have to read this book in chapter order. You can choose to read all of the Sun Room sections at once or perhaps only the Chapter Intros. It was designed with you in mind.

People who are going through something that is draining can find it hard to focus on improving their situation. Taking that into consideration, you can dip in and out of sections as and when suits you.

Of course, the book had to follow a loose structure if it was to make any sense at all, so you will find that the overall arc takes you on a journey from sallow to sun-kissed.

Whichever way you decide to read it, I'm glad you picked up Sunny Days and hope that somehow, in someway, you can be inspired to seek the sun for yourself.

The Chapter Introduction
Insight into what the chapter will focus on.

Perspective
An anecdote to assist understanding.

Application/Letter to a Friend
A letter from me, to you. My observations but also my hopes for you.

The Sun Room
Where you can go to find something to warm your soul, a quote, saying, poem or observation.

Balance
Mid-chapter clarification, often based on my experiences and

what I have overcome.

Journal/Reflection
How we feel impacts every facet of life. Answer the questions and perhaps pose some of your own. If you have something to work through, this space is for you.

Realisation/Letter to Myself
A space for you to be honest with yourself. A way for the soul to be heard - a conversation between your heart and your mind. Put your thoughts down. Make them real. How do you feel when you read them back? Even if we change or correct a line, paragraph or page, we have exposed ourselves to a level of self love and healing that only becomes real when we are brave enough to speak it.

INTRODUCTION

∞

This book was a work of pure love for me. I had been writing, noting and collecting thoughts for years before I even knew that the Dreams Days Collection would be a thing. Words had always been my escape, my way of explaining how I felt and why. I learned early on though, that not everyone understood my need to express. That was a tough lesson, partly, because I was being taught by those who bellowed, that my thoughts and feelings were not valid, but mostly because I truly believed that my feelings were not worth the time I was spending nurturing them, so I stopped.

Of course, now I realise what a load of fertiliser that was, but I spent many years believing that those who spoke loudest were worth the most. Somewhere in the back of my consciousness, I knew that this couldn't be the case and that if it were, I should like to change it, but I was completely out of self-esteem, so instead lived a life where my thoughts and feelings were constantly at odds.

As I matured, I longed to feel differently. I did not forever want to live in the shadow of others' perceived greatness when I knew that I too was capable of much more than the complete sum of my output. I knew the theory: I was valuable, I added value, I was valued - but looking back, I realise that whilst my head knew, my heart hadn't received that memo. What I knew, I did not believe. Instead, fear, insecurity and a lack of confidence dominated my character and I continued to behave as others thought I should.

The breakthrough did not happen like magic as the golden sun beamed upon my tear-streaked face allowing me to be instantly changed. If I'm honest, I am yet to completely conquer my fear, security and confidence demons. Yet, through it all, I gained the most powerful of allies: perspective. At some point, I started to demand respect. I stopped listening to those I had allowed to fill my thoughts with mantras of destruction. I extricated myself from friend circles that no longer served me. I took hold of my destiny and released it from the clutches of chains that threatened to choke my vision. One ray at a time, my purpose was illuminated and I started to see my life through the eyes of one who loved me: me. I put down the burdens that weighed me down and tentatively but surely, covered myself in hope.

Since then, I have had a million sunny days and I look forward to many more. Days where despite madness, pain and difficult circumstances, I notice the sun and welcome it to warm me.

I hope the thoughts in this book will remind you that no matter what you are experiencing, the sun will always shine. Take your time to notice it and see how your perspective changes.

From my heart to yours, Shae xx

1
YOU ARE

You're not as good as you think you are.

People often think that the opposite of humility is arrogance, or narcissism. They're not completely wrong. To be humble is a simple, uncomplicated state of being if it is grounded in truth. Anything outside of that is complex and can, at times, be quite ugly. There are many synonyms for humility, both positive and negative, because the pure nature of being modest in the physical, spiritual and emotional, feeds into so many other ways of existing.

Indifference can be classified as an opposite. It's one of the understated cancers of character that will eat away at any chance we have of caring deeply for anyone other than 'me', until there is nothing but a shell where universal love, care and hope should live. Confidence is another one which may be the most important of antonyms because it suggests an acceptance and appreciation for our own truth.

When we choose to face the obstacles ahead of us by putting aside our pride and utilising wisdom, we can achieve greatness. Of course, we must recognise that the air that occupies the space in between confidence and arrogance can be so dense that it can poison us with self-importance, putting us in a place where we only see our own greatness. Red flags should begin to sway when we become comfortable with the notion that our apathetic perspective is the only one that matters or is indeed the only one that exists, each outcome being flawed by the unfiltered air of ego. Our characters leak arrogance. We think that we are flying high but we are primed to fail and ready to fall.

Having a true understanding of who you are is a crafty balance between knowing your worth and understanding your limitations, between knowing where you have come from and understanding how far you still have to go, between celebrating your achievements and dreaming of continued success. It's humility that reminds us of the ways we are alike, whilst having the confidence to never settle for mediocrity. It is the desire to establish self trust and love whilst testing the boundaries of what is possible for you. It is realising and accepting that you're not as good as you think you are... yet!

∞

HOPE BEHIND THE CLOUDS

Her hands were locked firmly in place. She couldn't move.

She wanted to get up, but she was stuck, frozen in a moment that she could not control. Hope knew that there was danger all around, but in her mind, challenging her fear was a far bigger threat than the actual likelihood of death. She felt so small. Her insignificance intimidated any confidence she might have been able to fake and it left her cowering.

Cars were speeding past. Her tiny roadster shuddered as they overtook her stationary vehicle. What on earth was she doing in the middle of the highway!? She daren't look at the faces of those whizzing by. They'd be angry. She was putting their lives at risk too. She didn't want the responsibility of those lives. Her own was too much for her to manage, but her hands continued to be glued to the steering wheel. Unflinching, uncompromising.

Hope wanted to die but that would take a commitment that evaded her. Her eyes stung as she tried to focus on the white line that separated traffic. She swallowed often. Every sound was deafening. The blood rushing around her tense body seemed to taunt her. It flowed freely in her veins yet did not support her to mobilise.

She could not muster the courage to perform a simple manoeuvre. She longed for help from a super power. God, Allah, Iron Man. It didn't really matter. She just needed someone to tell her what to do. On her own, there was no way out. Her car had become her prison.

It had been 10 minutes since Hope had stalled her car on the busy motorway. She'd been making her way to work when her hands began to fail her. She knew what was happening. There was no time to pull off at the next junction. Heck, there was barely time to move to the hard-shoulder. She could feel her body giving up and with the last of her energy, she slammed her foot on the brake and readied herself for impact.

To the credit of the other drivers, they had not run their cars into her rear. They had swerved past, horns blaring, angry at her inconsideration. 'Stupid woman....!!'. Hope was unable to hear the rest of the sentence. The speed saved her from taking the insult and cultivating it.

Those traveling in the opposite direction slowed to look at the young girl who appeared to have parked in the fast lane of the M1. Their eyes scanned the scene for other cars and debris. They would see none because there was no accident. The spectacle they could see began and ended with Hope.

It did not take long for the Highway Agency Police to arrive. She didn't notice their arrival, as such, but she became aware of the lack of high-speed traffic surrounding the Smart car she drove. With the last of her courage, she looked into the rear-view mirror. She could see the flashing lights leading traffic. They were almost at a complete stop 20 meters or so away. She was no longer in immediate danger, yet the feelings of despair did not subside.

She had a new problem - an audience of thousands to her stupidity. People who would be late for work because she could not hold it together for long enough to make it to the hard-shoulder. People who didn't care what her problem was but who just wanted her to leave them out of it. People who would call her selfish, stupid and typical.

It surprised her to see a female officer at the window. 'Wind it down.', the police woman mouthed. The butterflies in Hope's stomach had given birth. She was overwhelmed with nerves and nausea. She nodded slowly in agreement but her hands stayed locked firmly in place. 'Are you sick?' The officer motioned again for Hope to let her in. Her knuckles white from gripping onto the steering wheel, she wasn't even sure she could still feel her fingers, how was she going to open the door? She wanted to but...

The smashing glass made her jump. In front of her, on the opposite side of the highway, a lorry had side-swiped a car. The car was now embedded in the central reservation and the passengers were stunned and bleeding.

The officer who had been trying to talk to Hope sprung into action. Her radio fed back as she called for help. Her colleagues ran to the aid of the crash victims and Hope was again left on her own. It was odd. The people in the cars behind her were no longer focused on her. The accident had taken their attention away and for the first time, her fingers released the steering wheel from its death grip. She steered the car over to the hard shoulder.

It took 20 minutes for the emergency services to arrive. In that time, two more cars had collided. It was pandemonium and it was her fault.

She was safe. Her car was fine. Now her anxiety had been replaced with guilt. She couldn't believe that she was the reason for other peoples' pain. Physical pain that was tearing through their bodies. Hope started to sob.

The tears would not stop. It looked as though she was crying from every pore in her face. Her blood still rushed, her anxiety flourished, the engine hummed, sirens wailed yet, amongst all of the noise, she could hear a small whimper. A child's muted cry.

Hope scanned the scene. Both sides of traffic were at a standstill now. The Highway Police had not had time to release those they had slowed for Hope's safety. Their patrol car still blocked the route. Drivers and passengers were out of their cars now, able to see what had caused a commotion on the other side but perplexed as to why they could not move along.

There were cars everywhere, many facing the wrong direction. Hope's tears had stopped. She focused only on the child's cry. Her eyes moved across the scene as she desperately looked for the origin of the sound. Under the truck - no. The back of the crumpled Corsa - nope. In the Range Rover that had been a barrier between the Corsa and certain death - it was empty. She began to believe that her mind was playing tricks when, just for a moment, her eyes locked on the tiniest hand holding on to the central reservation.

Between the trucks large wheel and the safety of the barrier, was a little girl that could not have been more than 2. Her unconscious mother was being treated by paramedics and no one had seen her. Hope knew what she had to do.

She looked down at her hands - one on the handbrake, one on the wheel. Her knuckles were still colourless. She willed herself to let go and one digit at a time, she took back the control she had lost. She focused on her breathing. One breath at a time, she admonished the fear that had taken ownership. She moved her toes, forcing the blood back to limps they refused to nourish.

Her guilt loomed but Hope had a mission now. She couldn't allow the knowledge that she might be the reason for this little babies' loss to prevent her from helping. The door swung open with ease and Hope made her way briskly across 4 lanes of highway to the place she had seen the little hand. As she leaned over the barrier, the tiny girl leapt up into her arms. She could feel the fear on her. Her name was Hannah. Her birthday badge clearly blinked, lights announcing that Hannah was 3 today. Hannah's tears were much like those Hope had shed shortly before. Her breath was short and her little body trembled.

Hope took the little one around the side of the 8 wheeler and towards an ambulance where she could be seen to by those who were there to save lives, not take them. Hannah's mother had come around and took her baby in her arms with such vigour, Hope thought they might both lose consciousness again.

It was all under control as she made her way back to her car followed by the Police woman who had initially tried to help. She was ready to be arrested. She knew that she had to take responsibility for what she had caused.

Instead, the Police woman looked at her briefly with a thumbs up and a questioning smile. Hope smiled and nodded back. She was ok. She would be ok. The officer motioned for Hope to pull into the slow lane and be on her way before she released the traffic. The highway again became a fast route for people to get from A to B.

Hope glanced back in her rear-view mirror. The ambulances had left. The recovery vehicles were moving damaged cars to the side of the road. The clean up was nearly complete. Hope thought of Hannah. The idea that she could have caused irreparable damage to her life lit a new light in her. She would call a therapist. Her anxiety would no longer call the shots in her life. She wanted to live.

APPLICATION

∞

LETTER TO A FRIEND

Dear You,

I see you. You walk around with your juggernaut of issues, weaponising it, honking your horn, conveying the message: unsteady vehicle coming through! You deck your truck out with lights, furry dice and memories from home. You know that you have a considerable way to go before you can empty the load, but you long for comfort. You want the weight to appear manageable.

You guard the contents as if your life depends on it and when people get too close, you apologise for the shadow your burdens cast, yet refuse offers of support to repack. You're a little bit defensive but shame is your companion. You know it well.

You arrive at pit stops and observe people with smaller trucks. They fuel up and leave, all while you're still trying to park. You wonder why you're lumbered with so much. You're aware that storage units are available, but your pride won't play, so you pay what it takes to fill the tank and get back on the road.

The road is long. The road is dark. The road is signless. The road is sometimes lonely. You come across other travelling trucks that look like yours. You get close enough to wave but you realise they can't see you. Your junk is obstructing the view. You resign yourself to solitude, convinced that you are not worth the effort it would take to clear the window. You can't see and you're lost but you keep going because you don't trust that your engine will start again if you stop. The navigation system keeps rerouting, trying to assist you, but your fears block the screen and you repeat the loop over and over again.

You do this for years, until one day, you decide that the price is too high. There have been too many near-misses. You check your pride and prepare to share the contents with those whose job it is to store valuables.

You reverse into a space at the storage unit, surprised that your juggernaut fits. You've had such a hard time parking in the past. You take a deep breath and release the lock that protects your secrets. The doors open - your shame is revealed.

You half expect the manager to say they are not equipped for this type of baggage. But those around you have kind eyes. They treat your load with care. They too had baggage once. They place each item into a clean container, secure and easy to manage but accessible. They assure you that you can visit whenever you want, but say, in their experience, the visits dwindle and the value of all that is kept diminishes. They tell you that over time, you'll no longer need such a big space and, they offer reassurance that when the right time comes, they'll be happy to downsize you to something more suitable.

You wonder if they really mean what they say, but exhaustion trumps caution, so you give in and allow them to transfer the pieces of your life. Some are whole. Some, broken. They are willing to take everything. You offer to keep some back but they say no. They know you're tired - you've been travelling alone a long time.

As you sit, you feel odd. The feeling is unfamiliar. You can finally breathe, no longer worried about the cost of fuel, free of the curse that caused you to value isolation. You wonder if this is what freedoms feels like.

Your truck is now empty but for one thing. A broom. You get up and start sweeping. The dust threatens to choke you as it whirls, but you persevere, willing the air to clear. It's hard work but through the dust and sweat, you begin to see the beauty of the trailer. Everything that was within has now been replaced by something more precious.

Your eyes well up. Release feels great. You understand that you must protect this space now. You don't have to carry everything you encounter.

You pick up your keys and get ready to travel again, because now, your vessel is overflowing with something much lighter: peace.

You are extraordinary. You are remarkable. You are free.

Love, always x

∞

MUDDY WATER

A puddle from a distance with the
sun beaming down on it looks amazing!
But no matter how enticing, beautiful or exciting it is,
when you get up close, it's just muddy water.

*Ensure that your character is just as
beautiful inside as it is outside.*

∞

CHOICES

We all have choices to make when it comes to figuring out exactly who we are and who we want to be. It is, of course, complex and never straight forward. The outcome is impacted by friendships, interactions, environments, experiences, health and everything else that life presents, but, your revelation will depend on nothing more than your choices.

You have to be accountable for the things that happen to you as a result of the decisions you make. Others have their roles to play in defining who you are and, you have your part to play too.

The act of driving can be seen as selfish because you're constantly looking for ways to put yourself first, to promote your own agenda, to fill gaps and to ensure you're getting to where you need to be. That's great for the confident person who is willing to pull out and join high-speed traffic. In fact, for those people, that action looks less like selfishness and much more like proactively seeking opportunities. They know that very few people are going to slow down to let them in, so they edge into the path of oncoming vehicles just enough to be noticed. Eventually, someone sees and slows down just enough to create a space for them. They find their place and close the gap.

Their style of driving works for them, but is dependent on others choosing to adapt.

Then, there are those who are too kind or too afraid to push themselves into what they perceive as harms' way. You see, in order to join the throng, they have to leave the comfort of the junction. They don't want to appear rude or forceful, so they stay put, believing that someone will notice and let them in. They hold up progression for themselves and those behind them.

Finally, there are those who are already on the highway. They are not duty-bound to notice incoming vehicles. The 'give way' sign is on the junction, not the carriageway, but travellers who have been doing this a while have faced junctions before so, they make space to let other drivers in.

The first driver makes choices that have the potential to end badly, but they are willing to entertain risk for the opportunity to grow. The second, remains safe, but stationary. The final, employs balance and insight which leads to success: those at the junction can pull into the stream of cars; those creating their own way rather haphazardly are moving forward, albeit nearly at other drivers' expense and; those already traveling can move into other lanes so that their journey is not affected, despite having made a way for others.

There will be situations where all drivers' decisions make sense but none of their methods will work 100% of the time for anyone without engaging balance. It's ok to give way to people sometimes but, if you make a way for too many people, you cease to move. Without balance, you struggle to progress on your journey and you hand others power over your progression and value.

Understanding how that balance affects you is important in knowing who you are, what you're comfortable with, where you're trying to go and what you're willing to do to get there.

The same can be said of self-love. The art of balancing the love we have for ourselves, with love that others require and/or demand from us, sets the course for who we become and, whether we will, ultimately, be fulfilled.

Maybe, you don't know which road you're on right now. That's ok. Remember this: you cannot hide behind ignorance - self reflection can be tough, as can pushing yourself out and becoming intentionally vulnerable, but those options are overflowing with rewards.

Nobody should want to be too much of any one thing. The value your character reveals is always reflective of the person you truly are. If you're compassionate, it will show. If you're generous, it will be seen. If you are cruel, be sure your actions will reveal it. If you are insincere, the sound of your inauthenticity will resound.

By denying others the opportunity to progress, you show them that you prioritise your right to bypass them and, you devalue your right to access compassion from them later on.

By pushing in on too regular a basis without a thought for the damage you may be responsible for, you cause people to swerve when they see you.

They begin to recognise the behaviour as being detrimental to their own progress and they steer clear.

Becoming an expert at manoeuvring without being a hazard to others is a skill that takes time to hone, but it can be done. Intent matters. What we do is important but why we do it, more-so. People will either stretch your vision or choke your dreams. More pertinent though - you will either stretch or stifle theirs.

You have a choice to make. Who are you and what kind of driver will you be?

∞

REFLECTION

Understanding ourselves means taking a brave look in the mirror and acknowledging how we really appear. It means being proud of the ways in which we excel at being human, but it also means admitting our shortcomings and being real enough to make a decision about what kind of person we should be.

The hardest part of being ok with who we are is realising that we are not the only people who matter in our stories. We have baggage, we have anxieties, we have journeys to make, but how we act impacts those who encounter us.

A wise person knows that for seeds to grow, they need a greenhouse. It's the same in life. We may survive and even thrive but to get the most out of living, we need to protect our growth. To build your ULTIMATE greenhouse, you need glass. The job of the glass is two-fold. It protects delicate seeds from the elements and, it allows the suns rays to nourish life. You need to be able to see through to the deepest corners of your heart in order to begin working on yourself.

As you conclude this chapter, look at the following questions. Consider how they make you feel. Be really honest. Then, settle down to write your own letter to yourself. Use what you have learned to populate the blank page. Start your letter, 'Dear Me, I've been thinking about....'. Once you've said all you want to say to yourself, signoff, 'I love you. Me x'.

There are 12 chapters in this book. By the time you arrive at the end, you should have written 12 Letters to Myself. Keep them safe. I'll let you know what to do with them later.

Reflection Questions:

Who are you?
Which is your favourite version of you?

Are you able to be completely honest with yourself?

Who do you become when you start to balance choice with opportunity?

Are you affected by what those choices mean for you?

Are you already on your journey, bypassing those at junctions who just can't find the courage to pull into traffic? Or, are you behind them, forcing their progress so that when they move, you can too?

Are you a junction-lurker or someone who gives way?

When passing others, do you tell yourself that they'll get there eventually, that somebody has to let them through?

Are you at your own intersection, gathering momentum to jump in wherever you can?

Do you pull out regardless of who has to brake because you crossed dangerously into their paths?

Who is the person in your life who gave you a chance?

Are you ready to put your load into storage?

Who do you want to be and do you know how to get there?

Do you want to change?

Do you need to change?

Are you ready to do what it takes?

∞

LETTER TO MYSELF

Dear Me,

2

VALUABLE

Type 'define valuable' into a search engine and you'll find the following: 'A thing that is of great worth...'. That makes sense, right? In an everyday context, we understand it to mean something of great worth too. What Google cannot do with those search terms though is explain subjectivity or relativity. Does it matter to whom the precious thing is valuable? Does it matter if there is no monetary value? Does it matter at all if it matters to no one?

As humans, this is where we often find ourselves lost. Our consideration of our worth is tied up in the value that others place on it - the amount that we love inward being unbalanced with the extreme amount we shed. There is a saying, 'You cannot truly love others until you know how to love yourself'. What does that really mean? As love is such an all-encompassing and complex term, it may be easier to replace the second 'love', with 'value'.

You cannot truly love others until you know how to value yourself. Suddenly it becomes a bit more clear and we are able to understand how it relates to us.

There is a saddening trend of titanic proportions happening right within us. It is the desire to impress, to garner approval and to please others. It is the loss of insight into what matters and the superficial need to fit in. Learning to love and value ourselves takes its toll, but the quest to succeed in self love is ultimately an invaluable journey that benefits every person we come into contact with.

Consider how strong a stalk has to be to support its flower. We usually marvel only at the flower's beauty, but without the stalk, where would the flower be?

PERSPECTIVE

∞

THE BREAK OF DAWN

It didn't take much to make her cry. She would shed a tear when the news reported a human interest story that touched her. Her eyes would fill to the brim when she remembered hearing that she had passed her degree with a First Class award and, God forbid An American Tale was shown on the telly. It was always her undoing. Friends and family loved that about her. Her tears weren't crocodile sized. Her eyes would just well up slightly.

For many years, Dawn had been dismissed as too emotional. Her colleagues and acquaintances didn't understand her way of feeling things. A strong woman was not allowed to be soft.

'Who the hell cries over an annual report!?', she'd overheard her boss quipping at the AGM.

She knew the answer to that. Everyone did. Dawn had become overwhelmed when Red Cherry Media's financial report revealed that, contrary to previous predictions, jobs would not be lost.

It was something to be celebrated and she understood its importance, that's all. She knew a few of those who worked on the lower floors. Losing their jobs would change their lives in an unacceptable way.

Dawn was great at her job. She suspected that being an exceptional Deputy Director of Operations was the only reason she was still employed.

RCM had head-hunted her 3 years ago and whilst you'd be right to think that a gifted person may be rewarded for their skills, her employer had other views. Dawn learnt very quickly that nepotism and reputation replaced ethics and values. Junior managers and admin staff regularly picked up the slack of their superiors without recognition or thanks.

The executive office was overrun with an incompetent and cold team who had no idea how to build a sustainable company, but who were well-known in the circles where being well-known mattered.

Dawn had taken a chance when she took on the role of DDO. Instead of her usual 6-figure salary at Cranbridge Motors, she would be taking home a package barely fit for an intern.

RCM was a start-up. It had been running for 5 years without much real traction or success, but with Dawn's direction and coaching, its focus on Lady Pods had taken the world by storm. Who knew that a repurposed shed could change the face of business.

Dawn had known. She had made it happen. Eighteen months after being appointed, her vision meant that RCM was floated on the stock market.

The success of the organisation was astounding but her need to be fulfilled was lacking and she started to look for new opportunities.

What could quench Dawn's need to colour outside the lines?

Her input into the company had not been rewarded and while she didn't need the money, it would have been nice for them to acknowledge her hard work. Dawn was becoming bitter. A new opportunity had to reveal itself soon, for sanity's sake.

Late one evening, the RCM team decided to go for drinks at the hotel bar not far from the office. Dawn hated socialising with them but felt that she needed to keep people onside. She would stay for 3 or 4 drinks, then would make her excuses and leave. She managed 2 white wine spritzers but most of the staff members moved on to another bar so Dawn took her chance and left.

It was summer, so the day had been hot. Many travelled into the office coatless or with a light jacket. Dawn had worn a tailored white shirt with a skinny navy skirt, kitten heels and a vintage Levi's jacket. She was almost at the tube station when she realised that her jacket was still gracing the back of someone's chair at the bar. It wouldn't take more than 6 minutes to get back to Q's yet Dawn dithered over whether she could be bothered.

The fact that the jacket had cost her a small fortune dictated her actions - she made her way back to the drinking hole.

Six minutes was clearly a lifetime in bar minutes. As Dawn walked through the giant glass doors, she could see 4 members of the board at the table she had just been sat at. Jack had told her that they were unable to attend, yet she could see them, clearly! Christian, James, Gabrielle and Kofi. Jackson, Tyler and Louise, the founding officers, were all talking at once.

Dawn felt uneasy. She was not the jealous type. In fact, she knew this was not jealousy but it made her feel bad. From the reception area, Dawn looked for her jacket. If she could avoid going over, she would. As James got up to reach for his drink, she saw it, right there on the seat of the chair. Her gut feeling was to say goodbye to her beautiful item of clothing - there would be other jackets - but she knew that was not an option.

The bar design was such that you could be seen from reception, but in order to get to the seating area, you had to walk around two partitions. The view from the table through to the check in area was limited because the big holes in the partitions that allowed people to see in, were the same holes that housed potted plants and decorations.

The executive team did not see Dawn until she was right next to them. 'I think that it's time we go rid of her.', 'She got Red Cherry to float, now it's time for her to go!'. The founders had clearly spoken about this at length. The board members listened and gave each other looks of agreement as they spoke. 'She is bad for the image of the company. You know, so emotional.'.

Dawn cleared her throat and spoke for the first time since arriving beside them. 'Hi Chris, James. Gabbi, you ok? Hey Kofi.' The table was silent. 'I forgot my jacket. I think you might be keeping it warm for me, James.'. James' laughed was a nervous one. He stood up and looked behind him confused. Dawn's jacket was no longer there but had fallen onto the floor. James leant down to pick it up and handed it to her sheepishly. 'Thanks. Don't drink too much now. See you in the morning!'.

Dawn delivered her goodbye expertly and spun on her kitten heels as she strode from the bar. She was sure that she was walking too slowly, but her heart was racing and she needed to remain in control. They would be watching.

The journey home was awful. She fought the urge to cry all the way. Did tears equal weakness? Did emotion result in failure? They were going to get rid of her because she cared too much and there was nothing she could do about it.

She didn't sleep a wink. What she'd seen and heard consumed her and she resigned herself to the fate that would present itself the next morning.

She was ready bright and early. The jacket from the night before hung on the door frame reminding her of what was to come. She spent ages sat on the edge of the bed but she wasn't coming up with plans or escapes. Her mind was blank, exhausted from a lifetime of defending her nature.

Every step she took toward her new hell burned. Every cell in her body urged her not to go to the place that her body was warned her about but she made her way, one step at a time.

Dawn had expected to be in the office way earlier than the others. They were what were referred to as millennials. They worked hard but did not conform to the historic rules about early birds and worms. They got in when they got in and worked until it was time to do something else. They brainstormed around odd shaped tables and had quinoa delivered to their desks in cups that looked like flower pots. They were fluid and allowed for flexibility - as long as they understood it.

They could also be cutthroat, dismissive and could change their minds in a very short instant. Dawn wondered which group of employers she would be speaking with today. As she pondered her fate, her assistant bounded into her office. 'Morning Dawn, you look nice. The weather is crazy isn't it? So hot at this time of the morning already. Let me know if you need anything - oh, and by the way, control want to see you.'. Control was where the founding trinity were located. Their unique office sat higher than everyone else's in the building. They had a birds-eye view of all that went on but made a point of letting staff know 'we trust you to do the best job you can - don't think we're up there watching you - we don't have time to do that.' Today, they clearly did. They must have seen Dawn arrive.

She'd carried a big bag into the office today. If she was going to get the sack, she'd take everything that was hers on her way out. She set the bag down and quickly started to fill it. They'd have to wait for just a moment. She was cleaning house. It didn't take long. There wasn't much she'd brought from home. It was a sad realisation. Even in decorating her office, she'd been careful not to come across as too soppy. The pictures of family, friends and paintings from god-kids had all stayed at her apartment. Her happy place.

She took the escalator up to see the trinity. As much as this was daunting, she really did like this building. It's design was unique. Had it been her company, she'd have done so much more with it.

They were all sat in Jackson's office. Tyler and Louise, at the board style table, Jackson, stood over his desk peering down at his Mac. Dawn knocked the open door. 'Someone wanted to see me?'. She wasn't sure why she posed a question. She knew they wanted to see her for sure.

Jackson sat down, his face now hidden behind his computer screen. Louise motioned for Dawn to take a seat and Tyler smiled her way. Louise started to speak first. 'Dawn, I'm sorry to let you know that your work here has been substandard. You have barely any input in the weekly meetings we schedule.' Dawn could hear words being spoken her way but coffee was on her mind. They'd not offered her a cup. Perhaps because she wouldn't be here long enough to finish it. Louise continued, 'I mean, you make people feel uncomfortable, Dawn. Seriously, the Comms team told me that they were scared to approach you with changes to the A1 project the other day in case you got emotional. That's not the kind of company we're trying to build here so I'm afraid, we're...'

'letting you go.'. Dawn finished Louise's sentence. She thought that it might have been floppy and shaky but the tone that left her mouth was strong and final. She continued, 'Thanks for your concern, Louise. I'm sorry you feel that I have not contributed enough to the company that is floating on the stock market because of changes I implemented. I'm sorry that you need me to sit on a bean bag in order to contribute to the weekly meetings even though I send you my reports BEFORE the meeting begins so that you can look like you know what the hell you're doing. I'm sorry that the Comms team are scared to approach their line manager with changes that their line manager needs to sign off in case their line manager has strong feelings about what should and shouldn't happen and, I am sorry that you three are so ungrateful, petty and immature that you had to make things up in order to let me go. I do wish you well in the future. I am looking forward to seeing you progress in this sexist and ageist environment. I hope that your pool tables and cool vending machines are able to support your progression and to you Lou,', she was on a roll. Louise hated nicknames. 'I wish you the most success of all. Breaking other women down as being too much or too little of anything is no way to encourage growth and acceptance. I hope that when you go home at night exhausted from a day of stifling your emotions, you feel that you have achieved something worth achieving.'.

Dawn was done. It wasn't the best speech. She wasn't even sure how much sense she had made. She should have reminded them of her value. But it didn't matter now. By the time she got back to her office, the glass room the next DDO would sit in, she was walking on sunshine. She had finally found her voice and taken back the power that belonged to her. There were no tears, no urge to hide. She realised that she had been so emotional here because she did not fit in. She was not welcomed for her value as a person, but by what Red Cherry Media could use her for. She had given up so much to do this thing but in the end, had gained her confidence back. There was a difference between being someone who felt deeply and being too emotional. She had always known that. She just needed reminding.

She sat homeward bound on a nearly empty tube car less than an hour after she had arrived at work. Her Macbook on her lap, she typed into her journal, 'Never again will you allow yourself to believe the value that others place on you. Not at the cost of your career, happiness or sanity.'. She had no job and many bills to pay but Dawn had been reminded somehow of all she was worth. She'd be alright again soon.

APPLICATION

∞

LETTER TO A FRIEND

Dear You,

There was a time when the terms 'get out of your own way' and 'stay in your lane' were popular. They probably still are. They're relatable statements. When the phrases were coined, they were new and fresh. A renewed way of expressing an age-old truth: we are the biggest obstacles to success.

You may have used them yourself, a reminder to get it right and not to mess up.

Some use affirmations to build confidence, others find it harder to develop faith in themselves but all have the tools. Working out how to balance usage is probably the most important aspect of understanding self-worth.

I'll tell you a secret: we are all worthy long before we're perfect. The sun does not only warm those who have achieved all they set out to. It touches each person who acknowledges its existence. Did you know that?

When your feelings are so acute that they threaten to break your resolve, get out of your own way - it'll pass. There's more than one way to navigate out of the forest, but you have to commit to finding a route that serves your purpose. You have to commit to facing reality and traversing the thicket.

The questions you face are not what cause the most harm. The damage comes from the ones you whisper, hide, refuse to verbalise and ignore. Those are most destructive because your inability to allow them to challenge you is an answer that speaks volumes.

Know that you can do what you thought you couldn't.

You do add value despite yourself.

There will be times when you need to stay in your lane but there will also be times when you need to get out of your own way, put your foot down and feel the wind coursing through your hair.

Your worth is immense. Don't be afraid to admit and experience it.

Love, always x

∞

WORTHY

The sun will always shine,
the rain will always fall.
Take this opportunity,
make the most of it all.

Tears have their purpose,
healing takes time.
Heartbreak is inevitable,
preparing you to shine.

Today may be difficult,
tomorrow even worse.
It will not remain forever,
once you know your worth.

It will pass as long as you believe you are worthy of healing.

∞

TRUE NORTH

Everyone knows that a compass is used to help plot a course. That makes sense. Compasses tell you which way to go... if you know where you need to be in relation to North. Every day, you encounter folk who seem to have their orientation all figured out. They know what they're doing, where they're going and why they are on their journeys. It can feel stifling to watch those 'experts' escape the dense forest when you don't even want to be there. Yet, here you are, lost, with both options and time running out.

You have tools: your trusty compass, a tent, snacks, water and other survival equipment, but collectively, it's all too heavy to carry. The burden is overwhelming. You need perspective. Something that helps you to place yourself at an advantage - but help is not forth-coming and the loneliness is almost tangible. The deeper you go, the more alone you feel. Reliance on your tools becomes inevitable.

Moving forward is scary and attempting to leave may put you in further danger, so you decide to get comfortable. Your bag has everything you need for survival. You empty it and search for inspiration. Everything looks promising! A matchbox, your compass, a magnet, some money, water, a tent, a sleeping bag, keys and a screwdriver.

You start to pitch your tent, but the ground is uneven. You try over and over but you fail because you believe you need help. You start many jobs but finish none because you're distracted by your fear. What's out there? How will you escape the dark?

The wind is blowing and it's starting to rain. You can't do this on your own. You can't stay here. You refer back to the compass. It points North. It must be right but your gut tells you otherwise. Your body tenses as you decide to move in the direction your

tool points but you pack up and commit to move forward anyway. It must be right. It only has one job to do.
Your reliance on the compass leads you further into the woods. Your gut screams louder but you hush it, reasoning that you don't have the energy or skill to figure this out on your own. So, you go deeper and deeper until you're so used to the dark that it no longer scares you. You long for light but the dark is what you have, so you make do.

You fail to realise that your tools are helping you to survive, but they're preventing you from living. You see, without reliance on those items, you would have been able to find your way home.

At no point did you look up. If you had, you'd have noticed the sun rising in the East and setting in the West. It didn't occur to you that the same tools you put so much trust in were the reason for your demise.

The thing about compasses is, they can be affected in ways that render them useless. They don't know where you are or where you need to be. They can only do their jobs in a limited way. They would only have helped if you were able to understand their limitations. The other items in your backpack interfered with your compasses purpose and you lost your way. There were visceral signs but you denied your gut and allowed yourself to be led. Something was wrong, but your doubt in your own worthiness affected your ability to trust your senses.

Humans often rely too heavily on the people around them to identify their worth. They share their trusted insecurities and vulnerabilities expecting to be shown the way to a safe destination but, excessive dependence on tools outside of yourself may lead to detrimental consequences. A strong magnetic pull can change the course of your life. Your tools can help you to navigate your way to true value but they must not be blindly relied upon.

Navigation is fraught with frightening encounters. It always was and will continue to be. You're bound to be cautious and tired, but persevere, hope and develop your internal skills to live the life you're entitled to. You'll go around in circles a few times, but you are the only one who can take responsibility for a change of direction. The things you go through may be grim, but it's imperative that you don't give up on the possibility of something better.

You cannot quantify your value based on your inability to see through the trees. We can only ever assess our potential. Worthiness changes as we grow. Escaping the forest of issues that keep you trapped is grim - but better awaits. If your perception radar is broken, you'll never view your potential as anything more than a crazy, unattainable pipe-dream and the forest will consume your greatness.

We only know who we are today because we were able to make sense of yesterday. You're here. You managed to do it. If you are struggling with who you are, making sense of the past will help.

JOURNAL

∞

REFLECTION

It's hard to pinpoint the very first moment we knew we added value. Of course, long before we were even aware that worthiness mattered, we added value to the lives of those who conceived us. In the same way, it may be hard to remember the moment someone first crushed our self-belief starting a spiral of self-doubt and loathing, but we all remember how those things feel on an everyday basis.

Choosing to accept and promote our own worth gives us the opportunity to challenge those who would take our life force to fuel their own worthiness. It allows us to share our sunshine with them, showing them that the rays of acceptance and respect are far-reaching.

To build your ULTIMATE greenhouse, you need a frame. The frame, knowing how valuable we are, keeps the glass in place and allows consistent osmosis.

As you conclude this chapter, look at the following questions. Consider how they make you feel. Be really honest. Then, settle down to write your own letter to yourself. Use what you have learned to populate the blank page. Start your letter, 'Dear Me, I've been thinking about....'. Once you've said all you want to say to yourself, signoff, 'I love you. Me x'.

Reflection Questions:

What are the true components of your value?
When people consider you, what do they see?
What don't they see?
Is your need to help greater than your capacity?
If not you, who?
If not now, when?

∞

LETTER TO MYSELF

Dear Me,

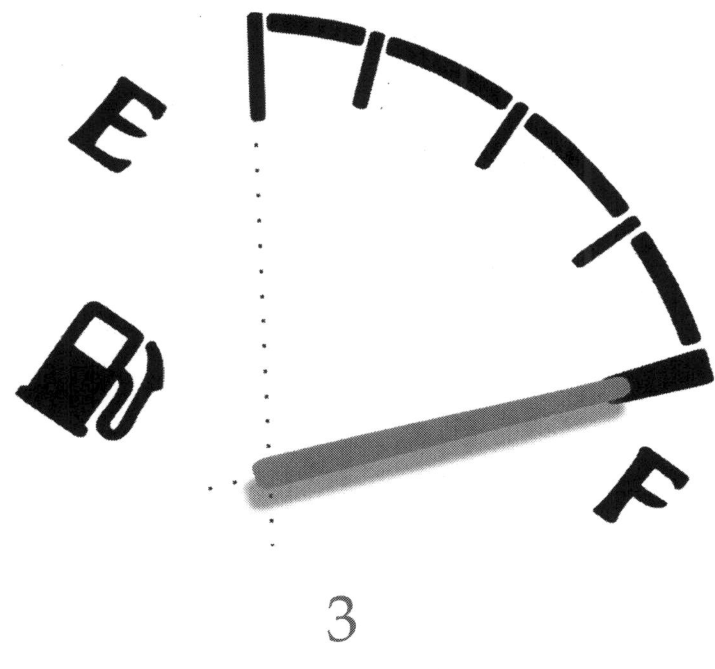

3

BEYOND MEASURE

Being your best or better than you were yesterday has been a buzz phrase for perhaps the last ten years. Everyone has heard it and understands its intent. But, if being better than the you of yesterday is all it takes to be great today, why is loving ourselves so much harder than it should be. Taking what we have learned about who we actually are and marrying it with the value that is placed on us by the pure virtue of our existence will start to join the dots about what excelling at greatness means personally.

How you measure amazing is up to you but is not limited to you. Our actions carry weight, our choices, consequences. When we dream, we begin a chain reaction of desires that help to create the structure of characteristics and experiences that we must take on and engage in to succeed.

Simon Cowell, Richard Branson, Oprah Winfrey, Steve Jobs, they all had dreams. Ok, perhaps those people feel far removed from you now and maybe you can't even begin to imagine that you could have what they have. When they succeeded, it was a different time. When they overcame their obstacles, the market was not as saturated. When they changed their worlds and that of those around them, they were not living with your limitations.

You're right. They are not who they were, they did not overcome what you are facing. But, they faced adversity and had to overcome their own struggles, trials, debilitations and hardships to live their happily ever after. They lived, lost and rose despite their excuses, environments and circumstance.

We don't need to search the celebrity pool to find inspiration. Your grand-parents may have fought in a war, your aunt may have suffered abuse, your cousin may have lost a child, your neighbour may be dealing with addiction. We can choose to measure our success by comparison or we can begin to live each day better than the last making beyond measure the only quantity that matters.

We must choose to be astonished by the minds of yesterday and of today. Those who created something out of nothing, looked at ordinary and decided it wasn't enough. The wheel, fire, instruments, advanced technology, cars, space travel, touch screens, flushing lavatories, paper, batteries, glass, bluetooth, toothbrushes, tools for surgery, electricity, money, music and so much more.

Those who came before us created the unimaginable and made it accessible so that our unimaginable would be easier to attain. Who are we to put a limit on what is possible? The leaders of tomorrow are waiting for us to change the world for them today.

∞

TO LOSE EVERYTHING

They were at the hospital. It was 4am and Mike was pacing. She'd been in there ages. What was going on!?

At 11:59, Grace had woken him suddenly with stomach pains. At first, he'd thought a glass of something hot might help but as he turned to face her, he could see this was not that type of pain. Grace was panting now. She spoke between pained groans and controlled breaths, 'Mike, get the car keys, damn it.'. She was not shouting but there was an urgency in her voice. Mike wasn't sure what was happening but he was happy to follow instructions.

They arrived at A&E 15 minutes later. The state of Grace's night clothes told the staff all they needed to know and they bounded towards them wheelchair and specialist on hand. They greeted them both by name - a fact that did not strike Mike as odd until much later. He was just so grateful that the fate of his wife and 4 month old foetus were no longer in his hands.

They wanted to examine Grace right away but she was doubled over crying out for Mike to be by her side. He was there. He was always right there.

Grace had been raised by many foster carers. She'd never known real stability, so when Mike met her, he knew that he wanted to provide what she'd never had. He was the man who'd be strong, supportive and silent. That's what he had learnt from media and society. He was to be the breadwinner, head of the household, corner-fighter and feeling-stifler.

In this moment though, he wasn't sure how to stifle what he felt. Were they losing their baby?

He heard the sound of heels. They came closer and closer. He knew the sound of that gate. The footsteps stopped just outside the private room they had been placed in. Then, ever so sharply, the door openly and closed. Grace's best friend stood beside them, as if by magic and Mike watched Grace's eyes overflow.

Miranda gave Mike a short hug and told him that he could wait outside. He did as he was told. They had been close since he'd met them. They were best for each other but over the years Mike felt his voice being diluted by Miranda's and in order to keep Grace, he accepted it.

He was now in the waiting room pacing. His smart watch tapped his wrist. He knew why. Do you want to begin a workout? He didn't but neither did he have the strength to tell it to stop. If he lost his rhythm, he might not regain his composure.

Room 21. That's where Grace and Miranda were. Waiting Room. That's where he was. He worked at busying himself. The consultant came for him then and he followed her back to room 21. Miranda was asked to leave and the consultant stood at the end of the bed looking sombre and apologetic.

'I'm sorry. You'd lost a lot of blood. There was nothing left in you to sustain life. You'll have to undergo a small dilation and curettage procedure and we're going to keep you in for a few days but it's ok. You can try again.'

The consultant left. Grace's grip on Mike intensified. They looked at one another. There were no tears now. Just acceptance.

Miranda again entered the room and understanding in an instant what had just happened, rushed over and launched herself on Grace. Her presence stirred up the room in a way that made Mike feel giddy. He instinctively released his grip on Grace's hand.

'Mike, I'm so sorry. This is just awful after everything you guys have been through. You probably don't really feel as bad as Grace, huh. Being a man saves you from knowing the true extent of this type of pain.'. Mike's grip on Grace had become loose, but Grace's grip on his hand tightened. She was not allowing him to go anywhere.

His mind ran back on the horrid scene he'd left at home. He'd have to clean the blood from the stairs, bannister and bed. He'd have to make sure that all was fixed by the time he brought his soul mate back to the place that was meant to be safe.

Miranda went on. He could feel Grace glaring at her now and it became clear. The reason the emergency room were prepared was because Miranda had called them. Grace would have found a way to let her know what was happening and Miranda would have made sure that everything was taken care of. Her light always shone so much more brightly than his. She was Grace's person.

She did not know this pain though. She was not the father of a lost child or the partner of a grieving wife. It was his turn to speak. Grace's grip had given him the confidence to explain.

'Ignorance does not save me, Miranda. I still hurt. I hurt because my wife hurts. I hurt because the fairytale has been interrupted. To lose a child is not one person's burden more than the other. We all mourn and we'll continue to. Please, give me a moment to understand this.'

Miranda was silent. Her guilt was written on her face. She knew she had been unfair but her nerves meant what was in her head would come out of her mouth. She loved Mike as much as she loved Grace. It was time for her to allow him to be there for her friend.

She kissed them both and left the room.

The heartbroken couple spoke about their loss right up until a bed was found for Grace on the maternity ward. They moved to the wing were happy mothers breastfed babies less than a day old and where concerned parents waited to hear whether they could go home after a miscarriage scare.

They spoke through the day until it was time for Grace to go to theatre and then Mike drove home. Tired and broken having lost almost everything.

His key felt heavy in his hand as he walked towards the front door. He could hear heels again. He knew that stride but this time it was softer. Grace was there to help. She didn't want his spot, she just wanted to help them to heal. Her offer of a coffee whilst he cleaned was a welcome gift and as he scrubbed the stairs, they spoke about how much they loved the person that'd brought them together and how they would all make it through this.

APPLICATION

∞

LETTER TO A FRIEND

Dear You,

I really want to share something with you. Even if nothing makes sense to you right now, it will one day. You may be broken into tiny pieces that can't be fixed. You may be experiencing the loss of your sanity, costing you any peace you thought you had. The way you're feeling is a result of being broken in a way that super glue can't mend.

You may get to the stage where the damage is irreversible. That's scary, but in time you will be a different you, a better you. Healing doesn't have to be familiar. If you change in the process of finding out about your you, then so be it.

In finding out who you are, you may choose to be different. When you finally find your safe place, those who love you will understand. Drive at a speed that is comfortable for you. Everything that came before may hold too much pain or need too much explaining, but find people who will be happy when you've found your peace, whether renewed or brand spanking new.

Seek those who have the capacity to give you what you need, but remember, they can only offer what they have to give. You have to apply what they offer in a way that is valuable for you. That may look like time, patience, support, resources, space or anything else you feel is imperative to your ascension out of darkness.

Find one who has the strength to understand the words you say and who can read between the lines without jumping to conclusions about what you need. Then, allow them to be there for you. Allow them to prove they can support you beyond measure.

Give them the space to praise you for the amazing work in progress you are. Use this journey to regain any control you've lost.

You may sit in the dark for a year and cry or curse or want to die. Allow yourself that time too. Figure out how to be ok with feeling and failing. What you feel can be ok. Give yourself permission to make it ok.

Learn how to feel and then figure out how to feel better.

Love always x

∞

FIND YOURSELF

'I suddenly realised that my inspiration came from
so much more than I could see.
I began to listen, to feel, to touch, to imagine.
My creative genius awoke then and
I knew that I was capable of anything.'

Find yourself and then don't let go of who you are.

∞

CREATIVE GENIUS

When I was younger, I went through a time of serious self doubt and character sabotage. I didn't like who I was because I hadn't yet learnt how to value myself, so I figured that I must be a bad egg. I was damaged and acted accordingly, but I knew I had a gift: I could identify with those who had experienced great personal trauma. I could understand and empathise without really trying. I used words to create safe spaces for people to express how they felt creating stories that focused on feelings I understood. For me, the characters were inconsequential - what they felt though, was everything.

Not only did I respect others trials, I seemed to feel and live them. I could sense immense pain and although I didn't have all of the answers, I knew how to be present and supportive. I recognised others' experiences because despite the differences between us, the emotion was unmistakeable. The lack of confidence, self-loathing and a belief that worthiness was not in my stars was something I could recognise in the slightest micro-expression. My heart was immersed in a well of pain daily. It lived there, so I cried for me and I cried for others.

I spent many years crying over things I couldn't verbalise for anyone but my characters. I hurt. I processed. I wrote. I identified. I repeated the cycle. I hated the place I thought I belonged, but didn't have the emotional confidence to escape it. My loved ones asked why I didn't step into the light but I didn't have an answer. If I'm honest, I didn't even have questions. I just had a feeling. I needed to stay the course.

My gut was my jailer and my saviour. It caused me pain that I am hardly able to recall in the same way now, but it also helped me to get through dark days, as it fed my tenacity. My dedication to bettering myself for others motivated me to remain in situations that were unhealthy, but when the shades came off and I was able to see clearly, I realised I was using the right model for the wrong reasons. I was trying to grow for others when I should have focused on growing for myself. The energy spent developing a 'me' that would satisfy a whole host of people resulted in emotional exhaustion that could not be sustained. I tried to design a better me and instead, lost all of myself.

However, amongst the darkest moments, when I would cry, I recognised that I would have the most wonderful moments of clarity. I knew reasons and had answers to questions. My pain unlocked perspective, so I committed to documenting how I felt. The skill of being able to write something that people could relate to was important because, when I became unafraid to face how I was feeling, I developed connections with humans I still love deeply today.

After years of living a life that was less than fulfilling, I started to heal. Partly because my heart is not made of elastic and was just about ready to break, but mostly because my mind could no longer sustain feeling as bad about myself as I did. Something had to give. I decided that as well as ceasing to continually perform checks and balances on my character, I would stop second-guessing myself and instead focus on loving me.

That part of the journey was long but rewarding. I started to stand up for myself. I was an expert at feeling bad and verbalising pain, but this new, visceral feeling of empowerment was giddying. I learnt how to embrace it and whilst I had regular relapses, I started to extricate myself from negativity, taking back the power that had always belonged to me. I had given it away so freely. To make room in my heart and head for confidence, I had to remove some of the pain that was comfortably occupying that space.

The process was powerful yet sobering. I found that I was able to experience true happiness by not feeling or focusing on the things that were trying to hinder my progress. The respect I demanded became non-negotiable and I felt more whole than I ever had.

With the loss of pain, came a loss of access to the things that had given me so much. For a time, I was too content to identify with the pain that used to keep my company. Recognition of trauma became harder for me to grasp. I felt sad because I knew that being open to feeling, mattered. But, I also celebrated the new experience of happiness that was becoming part of my legacy. I wrote less but I smiled more. I worried less but I thrived more. I acknowledged sacrifice but I made a choice to let things go more. I mourned not being able to go to that place to draw out pain as ink. I wanted to write but I figured I would have to learn how to be 'normal', writing about happy things and fulfilled lives. I thought that all of my creative genius was tied up in the limited view that looked out from the shadows. If I no longer had access to my pain, I wondered how I would create. I was now lost in a new, nurturing place. It was safe, but it was not familiar.

The darkness had gone and so, I believed, had my gift.

It took a few months for me to realise that the source from which my inspiration came was in fact deeper than I had considered. I hadn't lost my ability to connect. I had gained an ability to understand happiness. My experience had just become more diverse. I suddenly realised my inspiration came from so much more than I could see when the shadows shielded me from the glare of sunshine. I began to listen, to feel, to touch and to imagine. My true creativity awoke then and I knew I was capable of anything.

My ability to accept the dark hadn't disappeared. It was just better managed and understood. It did not seep in uninvited. I trained it to knock and wait. I learnt to be in control and whilst I still felt pain viscerally for others, I was able to access those feelings in a more healthy and uplifting way.

I had found and improved my gift beyond measure because I had embraced the possibility of losing the safe space the darkness had offered.

JOURNAL

∞

REFLECTION

Who limits how you understand your role in life? Often, we are the ones placing limitations on our capabilities. We get comfortable with knowing our roles and ensuring that everyone else knows theirs too. We make it our duty to police peoples view of themselves and we are quick to correct when their ego spills over into space we had allocated as our own.

If we trust that we are valuable beyond measure, we have to accept that all others are too. We have to make space to see others lights shine without allowing their glare to make our own insignificant. We all have roles that are expected of us but what is it that we should be expecting of ourselves?

Weather and wildlife in many forms can pose a threat to the work that is to take place in your ULTIMATE greenhouse. You need glue to hold all of the pieces together. Understanding that your value is limitless keeps the pieces firmly in place.

As you conclude this chapter, look at the following questions. Consider how they make you feel. Be really honest. Then, settle down to write your own letter to yourself. Use what you have learned to populate the blank page. Start your letter, 'Dear Me, I've been thinking about....'. Once you've said all you want to say to yourself, signoff, 'I love you. Me x'.

<u>Reflection Questions:</u>

Have you ever been excited to fail because winning meant change?
When in your life has winning meant losing something?
Were you willing to lose in order to gain?
If so, what did it take for you to make that choice?
Do you see people around you who need you to share your sun with them?

What will it take for you to find yourself?
Do you know how?
If so, what do you need to do to understand you?
What do you expect of yourself?
What do others expect of you?
Do those expectations align?
How do you feel about that?

∞

LETTER TO MYSELF

Dear Me,

4

LIVE

Live. What does that word mean to you?

For the longest while, I had no idea what it meant. I didn't dare focus on it because for many years, I felt that life was living me. I had no control over my decisions, not really. I was led by others, even though deep inside, I had views and dreams of my own. I had huge dreams that were drowned out by my insecurity. I stamped on the notion to steer my own life, previous attempts haunting me and instead I fought to glamorise survival. I attempted to make my life look like it was constructed from my desires. In reality, it was constructed out of my fears. A strong and sturdy weave that allowed no light to shine through. The dark dampness I felt each day kept moist by the tears that I regularly cried.

I championed the skills that I had learnt whilst surviving using them to gain great jobs and opportunities that I could not truly experience. I hovered over myself, watching the wreck become more twisted as I starved my dreams and valued myself less until I was powerless to become who I was destined to be. 'I can do this' became a common mantra muttered to steady myself instead of to affirm my ability. I wanted to be loved and respected so that I could learn how to love myself. If someone could love me, I would know for sure that I was worth a decent life.

It took some time for me to realise that I was harbouring destruction. I did not one day choose to live, change gears and smoothly transition from zero to hero. Instead, what I chose was much more sad and unimpressive. I decided that hurting was not worth everything it was costing me, so I took control.

Please forgive me for making it sound easy. That is not what I intend to suggest. I made that decision at one of the darkest periods in my life. There was no sun, literally or figuratively. I kept the blinds closed all day, every day. I spoke to very few people. I allowed no one close. I could smell positivity on those who intended to 'cheer me up' and swiftly kept them out of my lightless orbit, protecting my safe darkness.

But darkness cannot nurture growth and I felt ready to live life on my terms. I was blessed. I had good people around me. My mum and my best friend were understanding and gracious whilst they waited for me to find the strength to sit up.

I sat up and realised that I had yet more to give, so I stood. I stood and realised that the sun was glorious and without me intentionally blocking it, its rays reached every dark corner cleansing the damp and allowing life to emerge.

My choice and journey took 7 years and I am light years away from being worry-free or perfect but the decision to live allowed me to realise that the approval I searched for in the darkness would always evade me because, well, my life needed light.

PERSPECTIVE

∞

BATTLE ON

She wouldn't have been able to tell you the exact moment when she started to battle the urge to sleep. The speaker had changed. Doug was talking about finances in tone akin to the slow but rhythmic hum of a dryer. The room was humid and her eyes started a very obvious struggle to remain open.

The room erupted in laughter. She didn't know what had been funny but for 15 seconds, the tiredness was kept at bay. Her pupils dilated and she was again engaged, even if only for a moment.

She was there for a reason - to take stock of her life. These life coaches didn't visit her town often and she'd been on a waiting list for 2 years. She'd also worked a double, which meant that she was losing a very exhausting trial with her body.

A lone tear filled the corner of her eye as she again stifled a yawn. She was going to lose this fight and as stubborn as she could be, she didn't think she'd have enough energy to make it to the end. As an attendee, she would have access to the online version once it was released anyway. She'd be able to take everything in as Doug had intended.

The next voice she heard was from her dream. 'Emma, am I boring you?'. Dream Emma was wide awake. 'No, please Doug, keep going.' but Doug asked the same question again, 'Emma, am I boring you?'. The hairs on the back of her arms stood to immediate attention. This was no dream. She'd had fallen into a deep and obvious sleep during the presentation. In the darkness, amongst 499 other delegates, he had seen her.

Emma's embarrassment was real. 'Ah ha. She lives!' quipped the speaker, eager to move on. Her apology was barely audible but he knew she'd made it and continued with his talk.

'Many of you expected me to be annoyed with Emma. There are many who would like to have been here in her place, right? I would have been forgiven for testing her on the spot and asking what I had just said, knowing that she probably didn't hear it.'

The crowd chuckled. Emma did not. He went on, '...but many of us are like Emma. We want to be better despite managing, juggling and prioritising everything in our lives. We can only do so much. Ladies and gentlemen, Emma is here! Asleep or awake, she is in the right place, as are you!'

Doug wasn't to know that what looked like indifference was dedication but he got her. She had never met him but he saw her. He understood the struggle and her need to be present in a place that could change her life despite her bodies objections.

The tiredness was gone now. Emma was fully alert. The screen behind the stage filled with huge letters. B A T T L E O N. What Emma thought was a rod to break her became a lesson to motivate her.

Her perseverance had been rewarded with acknowledgement and although she was sat in the darkened hall illuminated only by the lit stage, someone had plucked her from obscurity and given her permission to be imperfect.

Of course, Doug knew her details because she had filled in a pre-entry survey as she arrived. He liked to know his audience.

Regardless, Emma had been moved by someone who saw more than her current action but who noted her motivation. It made all the difference and she again found the energy to battle on.

∞

LETTER TO A FRIEND

Dear You,

Put your affairs in order then go find the sun. Don't allow the darkness to take what little time you have left. If tomorrow is truly not promised, after the panic of 'I'm not ready to die', should come the understanding that you don't have to tolerate the dark forever or alone. There'll always be someone struggling in the same darkness you are but the sun will always rise - for everyone.

Put your affairs in order then challenge that order. Push the limits of its very existence. Change it to what it needs to be to feed your greatness. Figure out what you need, when you need it and recognise that those needs will change. When they change, push again. Upgrade again. Learn how to live, again.

Allow the tiniest interactions to change the course of your life. Be ready to move. Figure out what progress will cost and then work toward that. If courage is all it takes, pray for courage and then live.

Even though your body aches, give it all you've got.

Love, always x

∞

THE SUN ON MY FACE

I told you that you hurt me
Your response was 'get a grip'
I told you your words scarred me
You said 'get over it'
I kept my thoughts inside
Made things worse when I tried to hide
I wanted to appease you
but needed to please me too

I tried again to be clear
My voice you did not hear
I attempted to say it another way
You didn't have time for it today
I took some space to see
If I was really as bad as I seemed
You didn't notice I was gone
I felt alone for so long

I found the strength to take a step
Not knowing where I might land
Anywhere was better than here
No support, no one to hold my hand

With each progression though, I felt less scared
Knew my journey mattered even if only I cared
It was hard for a while, then got so much easier
I guess that's when I wasn't trying to please ya
I found my footing and took great strides
Building my confidence one brick at a time
My shoulders broad, the journey long
I had never believed I could be this strong

The sun on my face, sometimes leaving its mark
Remaining long enough to spare me the dark

Warming my bones, my blood and my flesh
Protecting my heart with a sunlit mesh
Deflecting negativity away from my soul
Using its rays to keep me whole
When darkness came and my cracks let in the cold
The sun repaired my broken pieces with gold

I continued to struggle from time to time
Remembering your words, as if they were a rhyme
Not meant with any malice but nonetheless, still hurt
Your tone clipped, your sentences curt

I nearly believed what you said
allowed your narrative to live in my head
but I found my truth, I found the sunshine
and I'm going to be just fine.

COURAGE

Is it true that no two parts of your life can go well at the same time?

In the summer of 2010, I started my own business. Life was ok. It wasn't perfect but I was trying and surviving. I had completed university as a mature student, despite experiencing some of the worst losses of my life. I had sold my house and had figured out what I wanted to do in life.

That was when I was diagnosed with Acinic Cell Carcinoma. My life was finally on track(ish) and there comes this annoying rare disease to remind me that everything I was working toward was temporary.

A short time after my diagnosis, the oncologist referred me for talk therapy. I had tried therapy before and was not hopeful for any breakthroughs. In fact, the first two sessions left me feeling worse than the surgery had. I cancelled and rearranged appointments, avoided contact and even allowed the physical pain I felt to overpower my need for psychological support. I had spent a lot of time in and out of hospital throughout my life and, true to form, my body was not playing the right game. My surgery had left me in pain, in crisis and in sadness.

Eventually, I managed to convince myself to complete the sessions that had been prescribed. I knew I didn't need to talk about why I had been diagnosed. I was never one to ask 'why me?', but my heart did need support from years of tolerating me berating it for being too weak.

These therapy sessions were different to anything I had tried in the past. The psychologist wasn't trying to force me into the pre-existing boxes she had labelled. She just wanted me to talk about what posed the biggest challenges to me as a result of my diagnosis. That was new. Someone who actually knew that the label on the tin might be different to the contents. The four sessions took me around 3 months to complete because I had been so against the process, but during the months following treatment, I realised that she had helped me to begin to identify the root causes for my PTSD. I had been living like a wounded solider - I had fought battle after battle but had not healed. I just kept moving through the hell that I had known, understanding that stopping meant death.

Speaking to the woman who made time to listen and who saw through the fact that I had already performed much of her basic role for her where self assessment and emotional intelligence were concerned, changed the course of my existence. It gave me options that helped me to consider living again.

As if I needed anymore convincing, just as I began to believe that life could be worth a dime again, I attended a hospital appointment and encountered a woman in the waiting room downstairs who was also sat next me in the x-ray area upstairs. That in itself is nothing to write home about. What struck me was the situation she found herself in and her reaction to it.

Whilst we were sat downstairs, she was smiley, jovial and even nonchalant. I'd heard part of the conversation she'd had with the specialist as my room was very close. The prognosis wasn't good. I really felt for her and thought that she might well be on the verge of a breakdown by the time we got upstairs. I was wrong.

As we sat in the X-ray waiting room, she was telling anyone who would listen that she was going to die. There was emotion in her voice but it wasn't fear or sadness - more resignation, I guess. Her tone said live, even though her paperwork said die. I knew that I would take on her sorrow personally and I did. It filled me up with grief and disappointment but it also motivated me to live the life I had left. Her attitude in crisis was enough to fuel a permanent change in my own.

I often think about her now and wonder if that was just a knee-jerk reaction or whether she was simply the kind of person to take everything in her stride. I'm unlikely to ever know but I'll think of her every day and hope to goodness they got it wrong.

JOURNAL

∞

REFLECTION

Deciding to live despite the challenges is a tough decision to come to. It is often signposted through woods and wildernesses with terrifying pitfalls along the way. However, changing our view of what living means can help to make the tough choices easier. We are going to live anyway, so why not choose how.

Knowing how to steer from the front rather than being led from behind can cast a reflection of light over the shadiest portions of our lives.

The sun can be harsh if not filtered. Blinds can help to protect little buds that start to grow in your ULTIMATE greenhouse. Taking the time to remember your 'why' and your 'how' even when the sun is not directly touching your life, enables you to learn, change and grow.

As you conclude this chapter, look at the following questions. Consider how they make you feel. Be really honest. Then, settle down to write your own letter to yourself. Use what you have learned to populate the blank page. Start your letter, 'Dear Me, I've been thinking about....'. Once you've said all you want to say to yourself, signoff, 'I love you. Me x'.

Reflection Questions:

Do you believe that once you leave, your mark will live on?
Are you actively working on your legacy?
How are you living (your best life)?
In your darkest hour, what do you need to hear more than anything else?
How big do your dreams feel?

∞

LETTER TO MYSELF

Dear Me,

5

LOVE

We know what defines us, how to measure our value and when to aspire for more but what about this thing called love. Choosing to give the love we possess takes the most out of the human experience because it is a commodity that we are not guaranteed to receive anything back for.

Imagine spending all the money in your bank not knowing when or how it would be replaced. Love is not something that is easily produced. In fact, it takes skill and practice to develop a healthy love that can be spent without fear of the deficit it will leave us with. Love is often thought about in terms of what it means for the person that feels it but an important aspect of this emotion is what it will do for those who are privileged enough to offer it. Those able to weigh the benefits as necessary even when they will be 'losing' will ultimately find love in the least expected of places.

This does not negate the saying, 'to love others you must first love you'. Nope, all it does is classify that both of those kinds of love as different. The value we place on ourselves has to be akin to respecting, trusting and revering royalty. What we share with others does not have to deplete the well that is used for filling us up.

When we are able to love ourselves as we are but also see a need for improvement, we have the capacity to nurture others' need for the same things, even if they do not yet recognise those things in themselves. We are able to show compassion, acceptance and tolerance to those who treat others and themselves, as less than.

Love is powerful and should be protected so, we often bar the unworthy from it. Think on this though: if we were to use love to build, despite unworthiness, without expecting gratitude, the possibility for life-altering growth would be infinite.

Of course, where the heart is concerned, wisdom is key. We should not allow ourselves to be used - but we must learn to share our love based on our capacity to give it, not others' worthiness of it. When we remove judgement, love has license to work its magic. Realising that the answers to why we ought to share are not always going to be ours to know, frees us from having to choose who, what and when.

Once we understand that we don't have to choose who deserves love, learning how to just be love becomes the most important of focuses.

PERSPECTIVE

∞

I REALLY HATE YOU

Chapter One – The End

Harley

Sometimes, I really hate you! Sometimes I really, really hate you! I haven't told you before now because I've only just realised it. After fourteen years of friendship and what was meant to resemble a relationship, I realise that I HATE YOU!

I know that the reasonable thing would be to discuss this with you face to face, but after years of being reasonable, I don't feel like being that person anymore and I blame you!

So, if you would do me the honour of accepting this as notification that you're a BIG, FAT MORON, I'll return the favour and never contact you again!

Kate

No date stamp, no envelope, not even a signature. Just a printed letter left on his side of the bed. After years of emotional abuse, I had finally woken up and realised that I was not happy. Oh, I had felt that way before, but it was always fleeting and if I needed a dose of 'you're just being silly', Harley was always on hand with a giant syringe to give me just what I needed.

As the rain fell outside, I realised that I wanted the tears to come so badly, but they were lost in a place that I, apparently, did not have access to. I had learnt to hide the pain of failure so well, that now, when I was allowing myself to feel, I couldn't bear the emotion that came with it.

The radio was playing sad songs and I couldn't imagine how people managed to listen to that crap night after night without suicidal thoughts!

'Why'd she have to go,
I don't know, she didn't say.
I did something wrong, now I long for yesterday....'

Someone pass me a shot gun! I was sipping cheap alcohol that tasted of paint stripper when my world stopped for just a moment - Daniel Bedingfield's 'If You're Not The One' came on. I wanted to WANT to stay, to mean the words of that song and to be able to apply them to my situation, but it just wasn't relevant anymore. I didn't want to be given a reason to stay. It was time to move on.

I had spent the first year of our relationship wishing that Harley would dedicate a love song to me. We needed an anthem. Harley wasn't telepathic, so the best I got was a paralytic rendition of Oasis' epic anthem, 'Wonderwall'.

That, Karen decided, was to be the opening prologue to her novel, The End. She had no idea why she had started it that way, but it felt good to be writing. It had been 3 years and 4 days since she'd stopped taking codeine for the pain. Her intention was to be clever and sensible by not taking cocaine, weed or heroin. She didn't want to be an addict. She just needed to numb the ache in her brain. It had taken 3 years and 4 days to understand that she was addicted to the oblivion she felt, not the narcotic. She was on her own and nobody really understood her pain - not even the drugs. So, Karen had quit.

Writing had become an unlikely saviour from her druggy nights and stressful days. Sat at her desk in the dingy room that passed for an office, Karen nibbled at crackers whilst typing. At some point, she mused, she would create an online account with Tesco and get some food delivered. This eating malarkey was going to be harder than she thought. Easily a size 6, Karen didn't always find the time for nutrition but a recent visit to the gynaecologist suggested that her lack of food might, at some point, impact her fertility - food won.

Three years of sitting in the dark, taking drugs and crying into fistfuls of Andrex had taken its toll. The tap of her fingers on the letters that were forming her book didn't provide total relief, but it would have to do.

She side-glanced her mobile to check the time. It was 11.55pm. Her fingers hovered over the keys but she already knew, the thought of that incident had halted her creativity and it was again invading all of the space in her mind until nothing else remained.

She opened YouTube. 'asmr whisper'. The search box was only too eager to comply. Her headphones in, Karen clicked on the first video she came across, closed her eyes and fell into a deep sleep.

The grating sound of the rubbish truck woke Karen with a start. Could they be any louder!? In reality, the sound was a dull and very distant rattle, but the stamp of an ant could have woken her the frame of mind she was in. She rubbed at her matted eyes, realising a second too late that the action would scratch and hurt her tender eyelids. Her chin was wet with dribble and her wrist was sore from supporting her head awkwardly on the desk. She must look like road kill, she figured, as she avoided the mirror whilst gathering her things. It was time to leave her excuse-for-a-home-office to get ready for her real job.

In her actual job, it was Karen's responsibility to be on the ball. She had impressively worked her way up the corporate ladder but knew she didn't deserve it. She was weak and fragile. A fake waiting to fail. With each success, Karen's demons appeared to strengthen, her accomplishments a teardrop in the ocean of her insecurity.

In a frame on her office wall, she'd commissioned some calligraphy of the adjectives that Rosa, her boss, had used to describe Karen when she'd been offered the promotion. The words were Karen's attempt to remind herself what she was capable of, but she was losing the battle. Karen trusted those words even less that she trusted China Ocean, her local Chinese take-away. As per usual, she looked at the note on the back of the front door as she left the house 'Remember, your journey to Loonsville has been powered by a series of very unfortunate events. You've come a long way. Allow yourself some love.'.

Good advice that's she'd forget by the time she arrived at work.

Karen could feel the subdued buzz of her phone in the bottom of her bag as she made her way to the car. Time to start the day.

APPLICATION

∞

LETTER TO A FRIENDS

Dear You,

A few years back, a friend and I went out to eat at Pizza Express. We laughed and really enjoyed our time together. When it was time for the bill, we motioned to the waiter with our debit cards. However, to our surprise, we were informed that our bill had been paid. A business man seated near us had been so moved by our apparent zest for life that he cleared our bill when paying for his own.

We were stunned, grateful and a little embarrassed, as we had never experienced anything so genuine and humbling in our lives. It was a beautiful and selfless act (especially as he made it clear that he didn't expect anything in return).

On his way out of the door, he told us that he hoped we continued to laugh like that for a lifetime.

I learned a valuable lesson that day: the world is bigger than just the here and now of where I am. Our words and actions affect people on every level. Who knows why our guffaws had such an impact. In all truth, it doesn't really matter.

What matters is that you are able to remember that your sun is far-reaching. Your journey isn't just about you. You can be someone's sun, whether it be because of your smile, a gesture or a look. Share what you have and allow yourself to be rewarded by others' warmth!

Make room for the gifts you possess. Work to enhance them. Don't get caught up in proving who you are to everyone else. Your dedication to your character will be revealed when the time is right. Hang in there. Acknowledge your fear but do not welcome it. Do not feed or house it. Do not entertain it. Do not fear your fear. Instead, understand, then deal with it so that you can make your way to greatness undeterred.

Don't allow emotional strains to break you. Anything that threatens your peace, whilst unavoidable, needs to be managed.

Learn what love means to you and for you, then let it radiate out of your pores until everyone you encounter is touched by love.

Love, always x

∞

SELFISH LOVE

Sometimes, people don't need you to love them.
They just want to be free to love themselves.

The day you learn that there is a healthy level of selfishness
is the day you can invest the love reserved
for others, toward yourself.

Believe it or not, your heart will grow exponentially
because you are free to share only what
you can afford to spare.

Your love becomes valuable
because it is not infinite.

What you have to offer is irreplaceable.

∞

LAZY LOVE

I spent years transferring from bubble to bubble, floating above my life looking in, not realising that the view from up there was limiting, not liberating. I had plenty of distractions in the form of people, experiences and opportunities but I was drowning in solitude. I wasn't really experiencing life. Instead, I was living moment to moment, my breath constantly held for an outcome I had little control over.

I loved the people around me but it was lazy love. I allowed them to love me in the ways that suited them and whilst, at times, that caused me pain, I grasped at it and held on tight because it was a drop of love.

It wasn't what I deserved though. I was worthy of an ocean full of never-ending love from those who had chosen me and they were worthy of unconditional love from me. The way love works is complex. You can't pay love in and receive it back. It doesn't ripen because it lives. It has to be tended to, grown, watered, guided, exposed to the sun and it has to be valued.

Inadequate attention to loving ourselves and those around us can manifest in various ways that attach to many of our life experiences potentially placing us in a position to fail at loving in an authentic and meaningful way.

Contrary to popular belief, love is not easy. It is messy and complicated and tiring and painful, but it's also uplifting, inspiring, life-sustaining and worth every penny it costs.

We have to make a choice about the kinds of love we allow people to share with us. Lazy love can work but if you are left with a deficit, this is not the love for you. Choose an all-in kind of love. The type that nurtures as it challenges, and then teach all of those in your orbit how to love like that.

JOURNAL

∞

REFLECTION

Big hearts feel deep pain but are capable of infinite love. Do you know how rewarding that potentially is for us? The balance between exquisite pain and deep, moving love hangs on such a thin line that we are bound to encounter both at various points in our lives.

Giving love the absolute respect is deserves becomes a gratifying and rewarding act that everyone we touch will be affected by. Loving others matters, but loving ourselves is the greatest way to learn about how it feels to really share something indescribable with another.

When constructing your ULTIMATE greenhouse, remember to build a door. Allowing access to love and care from outside of yourself and making a way for others to see how to take care of you, is paramount to your success.

As you conclude this chapter, look at the following questions. Consider how they make you feel. Be really honest. Then, settle down to write your own letter to yourself. Use what you have learned to populate the blank page. Start your letter, 'Dear Me, I've been thinking about....'. Once you've said all you want to say to yourself, signoff, 'I love you. Me x'.

Reflection Questions:

How do you love yourself?
Are there people in your life who threaten that love?
What do you have in place to handle situations that threaten that?
Are there people who are envious of your sun?
How do you react to/manage that?
How can you show them how to love and respect themselves and you?

What will it take to get you to a place where the love you save for you is unshakable?

∞

LETTER TO MYSELF

Dear Me,

6

BE WILLING TO CHANGE

Sometimes we can be selective about who we're honest with and rightly so! It's not every friend who'll pass up the opportunity to use your weakness against you. However, our biggest weaknesses are often revealed when we are least honest with ourselves. Being able to make self-honesty a habit, no matter how uncomfortable will always serve to elevate you. This self-honesty may lead to a realisation that a change needs to occur. What then?

A few years ago, I overheard a young and obviously newly-wed couple talking about Facebook. The husband, Alan, was gently but firmly assuring his wife that he had not 'added' his ex to his page and therefore should not be held accountable for anything she posted on his page. His wife, Emma, dutifully replied that not only was it his responsibility to veto each post made on his wall, but that he should also remove his ex from his 'friends', as this would prove his love and devotion to her.

I laughed as I imagined just what kind of couple they would become in 20, 40 or even 60 years. But my laugh became a smile and my smile, a grimace as I realised that there was a real issue at hand - who was in fact, right and would they ever come to a conclusion!? Was it right for Emma to expect that, with her wedding ring, she would also have the right to exclude parts of her husband's past as she wished? Or, was he right in thinking that as long as he was not the instigator of the renewed 'friendship', it was fine to have old exes 'find' him, at the cost of his new wife's sanity?

I needed answers, so at my monthly 'girl's night out', I asked a few of my friends the question and not surprisingly, they stated that they 'would be extremely uncomfortable with their partners being in touch with their exes', an answer I expected. I followed up with the question I knew they all dreaded, 'Did that mean that they did not trust their partners?'.

The answers were as varied as the ocean is deep, but with a common theme of exasperation at my brazenness. 'How could I dare link the two?', 'It's not that they did not trust HIM, they did not trust HER'. I ran like the wind to get out of there. Proverbial bullet-proof vest or not, they were acting like women scorned and they had not even met Alan!

I was no closer to finding the solution that would put my mind at rest. But instead of risking life and limb again, I decided to look closer to home – I asked myself 'What would I do in that position?'. I weighed up whether my marriage was more likely to break down because of my lack of trust or, because of an ex that was probably less of a threat to me, than I was to the staff in Next, during the mid-season sale! My mind ran back over the employee that nearly lost a finger during a 5am stampede and my question was answered. Not only did these women not trust their men enough, but they could not even admit their own insecurities. They appeared to not be willing to change.

I wished that I could find Emma and tell her to let it go, and urge Alan to be more understanding but in a lucid moment, I knew that she and Alan would obviously be long gone. I decided it was just as well as I am sure that the advice of a random stranger that had been eavesdropping on a lovers' tiff, was the last thing they would have welcomed.

Change can be uncomfortable but it is necessary. Compromise is a powerful friend if we can find the courage to face our insecurities. Alan and Emma were probably fine as are many of the other couples who have had Facebook issues since, but this issue wasn't really about their social media. It was about their willingness to change and meet each other at the dark, unfamiliar crossroad so that they could find the light they sought together. They had to be willing to face and embrace their individual change in order to grow as a couple.

∞

DEAR DIARY

Dear Diary
I have neglected you recently. It's not that I've been too busy, it's just that I seem to have lost the motivation to do anything remotely good for me. In fact, I have almost lost the will to breathe! (Note to self: find out where can purchase remote breathing machine).

At the beginning of this year, I was on top of the world. Work was good, church was good, family was great, my love life was.... all the same, I felt free.

Since May, something has come over me. Something that seems to have sucked the life out of me. The job I love has become repetitive, church has become irrelevant, my relationship with my family has become strained and my love life.... well, nothing much has changed there, surprise, surprise. I just long for some kind of emancipation from the cloud that I appear to have stolen from an unsuspecting pessimist.

I have so much to do and no inspiration to do it.

sigh Mind you, I do have the motivation to sleep.

Night x

Dear Diary
I feel bad. I don't socialise, read, exercise or pray anymore. What's wrong with me!?
.....
.....
.....
You're no help!

Night x

Dear Diary
My sister Naomi had a false alarm today. I received a call at 10.07 (5 minutes into the weekly directorate meeting) letting me know that my 17 year old unmarried sister was being rushed into labour 2 months early.

That put some fire up under me, I tell you!

Dear Diary
Guess what! I met a guy today! He held the door open for me as I was on my way out for lunch. He looked at me as if he recognised me from somewhere, but I would know if I had seen that heavenly face before!

I don't know why he smiled so sweetly at me though. Since I've become an advocate for the I-don't-care-about-anything-anymore-society, I've been walking around looking like a scarecrow.

Dear Diary
I can't stop thinking about the mystery guy. Perhaps I have met my muse!

Dear Diary
I think I'm losing my mind. I need something to believe in!

Dear Diary
Woke up this morning and still feel the same. Although, I am smiling a bit. I dreamt that I was a fairy that could make anything happen with a wish. It was the best feeling. I felt free again and in control. Life wasn't a struggle like my reality is.

In my fairy dream, I felt content, carefree and happy! Being good was in my nature and I was ultimately surrounded by greatness, as opposed to being shrouded in crap.

There were trolls and demons, but they were easily dealt with - I had the power to deal with them.

I'm awake and I'm sorely disappointed.

Psalm 23:1-3

The LORD is my shepherd, I lack nothing.   He makes me lie down in green pastures, he leads me beside quiet waters, he refreshes my soul. He guides me along the right paths for his name's sake.

Psalm 23:1-3

Dear Diary
I read yesterday's entry back and I realise that I sound pessimistic.

Sorry.

Dear Diary
Woke up this morning............................
Woke up this morning............................
Woke up this morning............................

So diary, I'm awake this morning, realising that I had stopped trying to see the positives in my life and in myself. I failed to see the good in anything. I know that I'm lucky to be here.

I guess that I needed to use fairy magic to rid my heart and mind of demons too.

Dear Diary
My car broke down so I was forced to get on the 77 bus. I hate that route! I ended up leaving work just in time to get all of the school-aged brats playing their music so loud that I thought I was in a rave!! I now know every word of every song ever made by Bruno Mars! and I've only been using the bus for one day!

Perhaps I ought to look at leaving work earlier? Hmmmm. We'll see. I'll decide tomorrow.

Dear Diary
As of tomorrow, I am definitely going to stagger my working times so that I don't have to travel with these inconsiderate children! Who dragged them up!?! Not a care in the world and yet they act like hooligans; spitting out of windows and shouting obscenities!

Oh good! My stop!

Dear Diary
I'm on the bus. I just saw a young girl being bullied by her school mates. She tried to ignore them until they got off, but now she's

just sat at the front of the bus looking numb.

I think her name is Sian. They shouted it enough. It's a beautiful name for a beautiful young lady, but I get the feeling she doesn't feel that way. I tried to hear more of the conversation. I wanted to step in and help her, but I knew that if I opened my mouth, her fate would be sealed: 'Ha ha – Sian, you got some old woman standing up for you!'. I can hear it now.

She can't be older than 14. I can see that she goes to St Anne's. Her parents probably pay for her private schooling expecting that she might have a better chance at a good education, but how can she when this group of idiots are making her life hell.

Perhaps I should go and sit next to her.
Oh, my stop!

Getting off the bus now.

Dear Diary
I feel so bad about not having spoken to Sian yesterday. I keep telling myself that the reason I didn't step in was to protect her, but that's just an excuse to protect myself from having to step out of my comfort zone. Could I have made Sian feel better? I didn't even have to put myself in danger. I could have spoken to her after they were gone; attempted to help. So what if I missed my stop! What if her home life was no better? What if this was the last straw for her?

I think of Naomi and the teen pregnancy she went through last year. She had me. Who does Sian have?

I can't write anymore tonight. I feel too bad.

Dear Diary
Sian was not on the bus today, either on the way to or from East Village. I did, however, see the bully-ring-leader. Her mother was punching her and telling her just how stupid she was. I couldn't see a reason for the tirade of abuse but it was over-the-top, to say the least.

It's so clear that our adult actions are being passed down to our children. The bully is bullied so she bullies.

What are Sian's role models like? Do they sweep things under the carpet? Who will Sian become?

I realise now that the lines between what we see as being a teens' reality and what is truly a reality for them can be blurred when we perceive it in adult-coloured black and white.

Ugh!

Night, dear diary x

Dear Diary,
Today, I popped into Zara to buy a few new items for work. The staff appeared to be incompetent and distracted. I was in the biggest rush and the store was more packed than a tube train during rush hour. I found myself being rude to staff and butting in to ask them questions whilst they were dealing with other customers.

I was fed up and the whole world had to know it!

When I got to the checkout, I realised my purse was missing. I was frantic!! I emptied all of the bags I had looking for my purse. It wasn't there! I ran out of the shop leaving the items that I had wanted to buy strewn across the counter. Not a word to the staff, who were sympathetically watching and clearly hoping that I would find my belongings.

I retraced my steps and as I asked cashiers in every shop if my purse had been handed in, I could feel the hope sinking from my heart into the pit of my stomach.

I gave up and went back to Zara feeling that the staff had probably helped themselves to my cards and money. I marched up to the counter and the manager approached me with a bag. He asked if I had found my purse. I told him I hadn't. He said that it was an awful situation to be in, but that he hoped my new items would help to ease the blow.

Inside the bag was £172 worth of clothes that I had been prepared to buy before I realised that I had no means to do so.

It turns out that the couple behind me had seen the whole debacle and had bought my items, along with their own, requesting that they be given to me should I return.

I felt so bad! They had probably seen the way I had treated the staff who were not at all incompetent, but were just trying to get everything done during a busy period.

I'm home now and I feel so awful about the sighs, huffs and moans. Despite my bad attitude, someone saw fit to grace me with something I didn't deserve.

Anyway, I'm waiting for a call back from the bank about my cancelled cards.

Night x

Dear Diary,
I just woke up and found a note with my post telling me to open my front door. There was a small box with another note saying, 'I think you lost me'.

It was my purse!!!

Even though I thought yesterday was such a bad day, it seems that it all happened to show me that even through my ungratefulness, the blessings just keep on coming!

I am sat here thinking back over the last few months of my life: my Mum's sickness, my sister's underage pregnancy, Sian, my work situation, my relationship difficulty (invisibility). The list could go on forever!

I have so much to be grateful for! I have no business being complacent about life and all it has to offer.

I want people to see in me what I saw in that couple and the kind

Zara staff. I am willing to change so tomorrow will be different.

Night x

APPLICATION

∞

LETTER TO A FRIEND

Dear You,

One of the worst things you can do for your sunny day is live up to other peoples' perception of you. Not their expectation, their perceptions. Assumptions are made about all sorts of things all day, every day. You have no real control over that. By the time you are made aware of those assumptions, it's already too late. But killing yourself to live up to them, especially when they're wrong, will dull your shine more quickly than limescale on a silver-plated rhino.

You too have to consider the types of perceptions you make and the irreparable damage it can cause for others. Have you ever seen something in someone that you know they're trying to hide? A defensive nature that belies their insecurity perhaps? Do you tell them that you see the real them and force them to 'stop faking', or do you position yourself along their route, ensuring that they have what they need to reflect on their feelings? Telling a depressed person that they are just sad, or a sick person that they should push through can be detrimental to the receiver.

We all need a little bit of sun in our lives but be careful that in trying to drag those you 'see' to the sun, you are not in fact flooding them with shade and shadows. Do not stand in their light to prove to them that it exists. Gently support them from behind, steadying them when they falter but encouraging growth.

We don't always have to lead, even when we have all of the answers. Effective supporting requires change and is a perfect balance of leading and providing tools that allow the others to find own their way.

Consider this: when we deal with children, we sometimes have to join their world. We play games with the imagined narrative, we pretend to drink tea from empty receptacles whilst conversing with stuffed animals. We understand that engaging children in this way helps them to learn, grow and enjoy life.

Yet, we struggle when it comes to our peers. When they have a perspective different to our own, we shut them down, letting them know that they need to 'climb down from their cloud' and be realistic. Whether commenting on television shows or someone stood in front of us, our tolerance is limited, much like our views.

You know what it feels like to be misunderstood and belittled. Take the time to change to ensure that you are offering the kind of value, support, life and love that you would want to receive.

You have more to give than you realise.

Love, always x

∞

EVOLUTION

Your therapy can change.
What you need can evolve.

What worked then may no longer serve you now.

Growth sometimes requires the unearthing of roots
but roots can be replanted.

∞

SATISFACTION

If you can't afford an attorney, one will be provided for you. That phrase reminds me of what it is like being a foster carer.

The last few months of 2016 were really tough. As a foster carer, one of my placements came to an abrupt end. But even before that, I was feeling lost and despondent. I faced numerous issues with the little boy that I ended up falling in perfect love with yet, I felt isolated and confused by the responses I received when seeking support. I was told over and over again that I was giving too much and that I would burn myself out. Each time, I explained that I didn't know how to give less than 100% and in fact, did not want to entertain a life where giving less than the full monty would be ok with me.

After the placement had come to a sticky end, I wrestled over and over about my role, what I did wrong, what I could have done better, who I am as a foster carer, who I am as a person and mostly, whether I was equipped to carry on. After a month and a half of inner turmoil, I was able to see that giving a different kind of all to the next child that entered my life via the system was the only way to protect my sanity and my heart.

There was no moment of joyous celebration though. I felt sad. Broken because I understood that in order to succeed, I had to fail at giving my version of all. Just like a court appointed attorney, I had to play to win without losing my integrity, yet I was tasked with maintaining my dedication at all times on minimal pay and even less respect. I had to fight for the children in my care without fighting with the system. Gain their trust whilst at the same time, introducing boundaries. I had to go against my feelings to be crowned a victor at the summit of my efforts. Like a public defender, I too was working to save a life. I had to keep going.

So, although those months had been tough, with a new

understanding of how I felt about my role in the social care machine, I reminded myself that I am like an attorney, fighting for two lives: mine and the child's and that my ultimate goal was to save lives.

I still think of my placement most days, but I think that he was my first experience of how easy it can be to feel like a failure in this type of work. I am thankful that I will never forget what he taught me and what I, hopefully, taught him, and I understand that satisfaction is multi-faceted and unique to the person experiencing it.

JOURNAL

∞

REFLECTION

Change can be tough. Learning to grow through all we go through is an experience that no person should have to accept but, it's life! So far in Sunny Days, we've learned how to identify who we are, understand that we are worthy of more than we had imagined, we've focused on how to keep moving in a world of obstacles and considered love.

This chapter addressed the terrifying theme of change and asked you to figure out the right time to seek and receive advice that leads to positive change.

It's in our willingness to improve that we will finally find the courage to make it happen. We need to be prepared to hold the mirror up and take a look. What we see may scare us but as an artist needs to see the tools required to craft, we need to clearly see what we have to work with.

Not everything in your ULTIMATE greenhouse will need the same focus, love or attention. Ensure you have shelves that can house things that are no longer needed or that you need to take a break from. The sun can still reach items stored safely away but they will not pose a tripping hazard.

As you conclude this chapter, look at the following questions. Consider how they make you feel. Be really honest. Then, settle down to write your own letter to yourself. Use what you have learned to populate the blank page. Start your letter, 'Dear Me, I've been thinking about....'. Once you've said all you want to say to yourself, signoff, 'I love you. Me x'.

Reflection Questions:

How do you decide what to keep and what to improve?
Do other peoples' opinions of you really matter to you?

How can you accept advice without it damaging your confidence irreparably?
How do you get over what 'was' and prepare to replace it is what 'is'?

∞

LETTER TO MYSELF

Dear Me,

7

EVERYTHING

Last night, I watched a movie that kept me thoroughly engaged from start to finish. At the end of the film, I felt that I had been given every element necessary to make a fair assessment of the characters and their relationships with each other. Had an examiner been waiting to test me on the life and times of said characters, I would have confidently passed!

However, because it was a DVD, after a minute or two of idle time, the screen reverted back to the main menu and I was faced with some options. I chose to re-watch the movie with an audio commentary from the writers and actors because, well, I was avoiding getting on with the work I should have been doing and as a creative, time spent watching the fruits of other creatives' labours can always be classified as research.

From the outset, I realised that what I thought I knew about the characters was a teardrop in the ocean compared to the full back-story. As I continued to watch, the film became extremely multi-faceted; the scenarios and interactions, having an even deeper impact on me the second time around. The big picture I thought I had been exposed to, was constantly being enhanced.

It got me thinking about the way we interact with others. We only know what is laid before us or what we have been privy to, yet we often feel qualified to make judgments based on tid-bits of knowledge. Re-watching the film reminded me that every person has a back-story that informs their actions. Their reasons for doing the things they do, may not be clear to us and unlike with a helpful DVD menu, we may never get the option to understand their actions.

Having concentrated on character, value, going the extra mile, choosing life, loving unreservedly and being willing to change, we have to be sure that when we consider others' circumstances, we aren't applying principles that only apply to ourselves. Displaying trust, patience and friendship gives people an opportunity to reveal themselves to us in a way and at a time that suits them, thereby opening our minds and exchanging our big picture for the bigger picture. Sacrificing what we think we know for the understanding that we may never know everything may be the only thing that sets us apart from the judgmental and aligns us with the misunderstood.

PERSPECTIVE

∞

ALL SHE HAD

The vista of Central Park out of her 75th floor office window was beautiful. She should be working but she was reclining in her director's chair, the seams of her expensive suit stretched to match the contours of her body. The office phone rang - once... twice... her PA picked up... 'Red Cherry Communications, Executive Office....'. She waited, expecting Lucy to announce a caller, but there is no announcement. As per usual, Lucy had perfectly redirected the time-wasters.

Her diary was as full as her bank account and she shook herself into action as she heard her fourth appointment of the day introduce themselves in the Executive reception.

She was content; excessively happy because the dream she had had many years before had finally come true and all it cost her was...

...nothing yet.

It's still just a dream.

It didn't feel great, being sat on reception in her real job, in the real world visualising an imaginary success. Back she went to reality as the notification on her mobile screen reminded her that her phone bill was overdue.

She let her mind wonder: just what would she give for that level of success? She would give up all of her spare time for a year if success was guaranteed. She would live in the gutter for a month, if success was guaranteed. Of course, she knew that nothing in life was certain, but really did wonder what she would sacrifice to make her dream, her reality.

All she knew, in the end, was that she had to work as hard as necessary to be the best that she could be. Then, if she achieved all she wanted to, great - but if she didn't, at least she have given it everything she had.

After all, no regrets. She had many more dreams.

APPLICATION

∞

LETTER TO A FRIEND

Dear You,

I was just having a conversation with a friend who is feeling really low right now. I totally identified!

We discussed all sorts of reasons and potential solutions to combat the feeling, but the only real truth that I could come up with was that feeling broken has its place in our development.

There will be times when you feel as if you're going around in circles, but each circle will bring you closer to the solution, even if you are not yet privy to what that is.

When you're stuck in a river being chased by a crocodile, don't stop to examine how you are going to escape - swim with all your might to survive!

Even if you don't know how, try your hardest to flail those arms and legs! It's all about survival. Only when you're finally safe will you have time to turn back and realise just how close you were to the jaws of death.

When you go through low moments, there's not always a need to break it down and find the cause. Sometimes, you just need to let the healing run its course, because if it doesn't weaken or break you, it will surely strengthen you. Leave the assessment for when you are better equipped to handle it.

Dedicate your ambition to seeing the big picture.

You've got this!

Love, always x

∞

THE RULE

I think about things a lot in terms of
whether I'm the exception or the rule.

If we're the exception, then we're working to ensure
that we are or are not negative something.

If we are the rule though, we need to ensure
that being the rule isn't detrimental to ourselves,
the people around us or even humanity.

Make the exception the rule and then be that.

∞

FULL CIRCLE

I've tried so many things to relieve pain. The manifestation of some relief though, is what happened when I reached hell and felt that I couldn't 'do it' anymore. I became almost nonchalant about it. That indifference was being forged with each tear and year, with each insensitive question from a family member and each judgmental response from someone who didn't understand. It's not that the pain disappeared, I just became expert at juggling a partly fulfilling life with discomfort.

It took 4 years, 2 surgeries and a lot of complications to get to this place. I still have pain that will always be there, but when I consider that it will always be there as the result of a life-saving-life-altering surgery, my perspective changes!

When you're still in the really early stages of recovery, my revelations may sound horrific, like you still have so far to go, but in fact, I mean it to have the opposite affect: there is hope for improvement. Nerves settle, swellings reduce and complications are addressed. They may not disappear completely and the process may feel as though it takes a lifetime, but our amazing bodies adapt.

People who have endured mental and physical pain will tell you time and time again that they feel like they're a drain on family and friends. I've felt that way too (and sometimes still do). Recovery takes a long, long time. We ought to give ourselves the space to mourn what we've lost (a relatively pain-free life perhaps?) and to acknowledge the truly frightful thing we've been through.

It's probably fair to say that we are not the same physiologically, emotionally, spiritually or physically. Learning to take things one minute, hour or day at a time is cliché but invaluable.

I've learnt that whilst time can heal, we have to accept that emotional healing does not mean perfection. We learn to allow ourselves to be ok with not being ok. As you embark on your journey back from hell, try to put your needs first. Consider perhaps, that acceptance could be a step closer to experiencing an authentic cheerfulness.

It's often in the detours we take in life that we find our calling. Your destiny may be waiting for you in a dark alley that looks scary and dangerous but you may be the person to fix the broken light so that others who must walk that route after you can finally see and be encouraged by the light you leave.

JOURNAL

∞

REFLECTION

Challenging everything you know or thought you knew will take you right to the edge of being broken. It will be easy at this stage to say nope - you were fine as you were, and crawl back into darkness, familiar and safe.

Fight that urge. When you exchange everything old, you are able to fill the space with items that better fit. Your old habits, excuses and crutches become magnets that keep you feeling musty. Refresh your life, everything has to go.

Your ULTIMATE greenhouse will need fresh air to circulate. Being able to feel and see the sun is great but you need a cool breeze to come in and replace stagnant odours that are lingering around your young fruit.

As you conclude this chapter, look at the following questions. Consider how they make you feel. Be really honest. Then, settle down to write a letter to yourself. Use what you have learned to populate the blank page. Start your letter, 'Dear Me, I've been thinking about....'. Once you've said all you want to say to yourself, signoff, 'I love you. Me x'.

Reflection Questions:

What could you do with replacing in your life?
Are you afraid of change?
What do you have to gain?
Do your secrets bind you?
If you were to go full circle, where would you begin and end?
What would be different this time?

∞

LETTER TO MYSELF

Dear Me,

8

ON THE ROAD TO HERE

One of the most rewarding roles I have ever had is becoming a learning mentor.

I was never the best student in school. My report card always said the same thing: 'Shae is bright, but often can be found daydreaming. If she can apply herself, she has so much potential. Shae just needs to focus long enough to realise it.'. Of course, those statements always filled me with sorrow. At the time, I believed that I was doing my best. My understanding of myself was that I clearly wasn't as bright as everyone thought.

That sad reality followed me through early education to college and at the age of 18, I decided that university was not calling somebody like me. I entered the world ready to accept my mediocrity.

I learnt much of what I know now in my first few jobs. Tenacity, dedication, finding motivation, knowing how to do my best, holding myself accountable for anything less than excellent.

Although it has been many years since anybody has described me as 'bright but uncommitted', those report cards had a lasting effect on my ability to understand how I learn and motivated me to encourage others to do the same. Nine years after deciding that I would forge my way somewhere, somehow as long as education was as far from the picture as possible, I found my guts and enrolled on a degree course as a mature student.

I had learnt so much about myself that I knew what I had to lose. I was willing to pay for my education with sweat, tears and every minute I had to give. I studied whilst working 3 jobs, paying a mortgage, volunteering and experiencing debilitating health issues. Knowing what that degree could afford me meant that I was able to engage in my learning in a way that I had never before been able.

University was terrifying and edifying. I learnt academically and socially. I challenged what I thought I knew and accepted what I found. I sought answers elsewhere when tutors who were better suited to teaching PHD courses confused my cohort and left us no wiser to what was expected of us. But I navigated the road and upon completion recognised the overwhelming sum of everything I had achieved despite the odds. My understanding had been expanded and I knew what I needed to do.

At 29 years of age, I had finally found the secret to being a great student. I had to want to succeed more than I was ok with accepting failure. I had to be unafraid to ask questions. I had to eradicate excuses from my plan. I had to remember what I was aiming to achieve. I had to know my limitations and then, I had to exceed them.

Whilst those rules did not apply to everyone in the same way, I realised that not everyone was able to understand or comprehend what was required of them in the way that years of feeling inadequate in the workforce had taught me. So I put my understanding to good use and began to offer support.

The results spoke for themselves and I made it a career out of supporting students who needed clarity.

∞

GET COMFORTABLE

She chose that seat because it looked so comfortable. It was the only one of its kind in the canteen and just like the last table in busy coffee shop during rush hour, she thought she'd been lucky to have grabbed it. After an hour of loud eating and nauseating smells, Tasha realised why the 'best seat in the house' had been available. No one else wanted it.

She made her way home. It's where she wanted to be physically at least, but she was avoiding Mercedes. The house was quiet as she entered. She must have gone out.

Tasha sat at her desk. She'd been creating here for years. Her body seemed to have been made for that chair. She took a deep breath and started to draw. She loved working in this room. Everything was perfect.

Her hands hovered over her art tools after an hour of drawing. Tea or Pepsi, she considered. It didn't really matter, both were within arms reach. She swivelled full circle swiping up the can that she had placed on the bookcase behind her as she rotated. A TV was on in the distance, someone was watching The Good Wife. Tasha liked The Good Wife.

The already empty can sat on the desk beside her tablet as she started to draw again. Maybe she'd last an hour and a half this time.

Hold on! The Good Wife! Who was watching The Good Wife? Had Mercedes returned without her noticing? Tasha had thought that she was avoiding Mercedes. In reality, she knew that Mercedes was probably avoiding her.

She had a choice to make. Get up and disrupt her relative comfort or stay seated, work hard and risk alienating Mercedes further. The decision was easy. She got out of her seat quietly, tiptoed over to the door and without a creak, closed it. She wanted to work on Mercedes' surprise.

None of the choices felt like perfection. So she chose the option that would offer the best reward. Whether Mercedes accepted her apology or not, Tasha was going to try.

APPLICATION

∞

LETTER TO A FRIEND

Dear You,

I'm sat in bed right now listening to the radio. I'm meant to be writing. I want to write. Instead, I'm thinking about the struggle you are battling in your war against sadness. I'm encouraged because I know that you're amazing, especially when you don't feel like you are.

I am excited because I know your potential and believe that you can make it through despite feeling like this today.

I'm hopeful because you've gotten to this point in your journey and although not everyone understands the way you struggle to trust, I know that they are capable of supporting it.

I feel warmth because although what you're feeling may be positively exhausting, I have faith that you can make sense of everything you have experienced to this point.

I advocate for your right to feel every emotion that occurs as a result of trauma and, I cannot wait for the day when I can share in your success and celebrate your better place.

My heart goes out to you.

Love, always x

∞

KEEP GOING

Sometimes faith can look like stupidity
to those who don't believe.
Dreams aren't made of fluffy clouds and rainbows.
They're often made of nightmares and heartache.
That's what makes them worth working and waiting for.

Have faith.
You can do it!

There's no point in stopping now!

∞

SOME DREAMS

For every challenge that is overcome, there is a reason to celebrate. I believe that there are those who have never had to appreciate the fact that they can walk 2 metres without any effort. Tell a man who has to learn how to walk again that each step is insignificant.

There will be times when people around you do not celebrate your small wins and instead admonish you for not conquering your pain. They do not have to contend with your tears today, nor your trials tomorrow. They are yours to ignore, celebrate or acknowledge.

There are so many who are bullied into submission and who don't have the courage or support to reconsider defeat.

You've got to chase the light. Get in your vehicle and track it down like a hound on heat. You will find your purpose entangled in that light.

The purpose I found took 3 years to reveal itself. Before that, I was depressed, faking moments of happiness or sanity for those on the outside. Even then, I was unable to sustain those moments because I was so broken inside. I was on 40+ tablets a day which did not help my state of mind nor my physiological health.

I found a way to work through. I imagined my life as a song - beautiful in its creation yet messy and unlikeable to the ear. Nothing to fall in love with until the notes, words, timings and structure had all come together.

A derelict house in disrepair looks daunting to the eye but the sun brings life despite that. Trees and plants still grow around the destruction.

Although I am in a very different place now, I still have dark days where I could so easily go back to the dungeon I clawed my way out of.

I would be lying if I said life wasn't still hard at times and I often question whether I am crazy or just misunderstood but, I have learned how to take my dreams seriously, how to put them first, how to acknowledge, learn and grow.

Your dark place may have derailed your life so very completely. It may feel like that for a long time as each minute of each day seems to take forever to pass, but I hope that soon you will get close enough to some light so that it can cast rays of hope over your brokenness.

Some dreams don't come true and others are ever-evolving. It doesn't matter which you have, as long as you keep dreaming.

JOURNAL

∞

REFLECTION

Darkness is not all bad. It is necessary for growth. Plunging into despair can provide cleansing and clarity as long as we know what to do when we are in a sunken place.

Soil and a solid foundation are an integral part of designing the ULTIMATE greenhouse. Planting seeds firmly in the dark and allowing them to seek the light to create a strong, powerful bond with the suns rays is incomparable to anything else. Accept that darkness will be a part of your story.

As you conclude this chapter, look at the following questions.
Consider how they make you feel. Be really honest. Then, settle down to write your own letter to yourself. Use what you have learned to populate the blank page. Start your letter, 'Dear Me, I've been thinking about....'. Once you've said all you want to say to yourself, signoff, 'I love you. Me x'.

<u>Reflection Questions:</u>

Are you afraid of your dark?
Do you know what to do when you're in that place?
Do you have anyone to help you?
What will it take for you to keep going?
Are you ready for the journey of your life?
How do you sustain through the pain?
When do you compromise?

∞

LETTER TO MYSELF

Dear Me,

9

BY ANY MEANS NECESSARY

There are so many opportunities to start over in a year. There are birthdays, there's Easter, Christmas, Lent, Valentine's, New Years, and of course, the beginning of every month. We have no excuse not to improve. We are afforded chance after chance to live our dreams and reinvent ourselves. We allow tomorrows to become yesterdays without improvement and we satisfy ourselves with meagre offerings. Our efforts dwindle with time and we begin to believe the lies we share about why 'tomorrow will be the day for change'. But tomorrow is silent, today is here and the emptiness of yesterday, a perpetual pattern of promise-scented mediocrity, is deafening.

We quote Malcolm X's 'By Any Means Necessary',
'I don't believe in violence, that's why I want to stop it. And you can't stop it with love, not love of those things down there. No! So, we only mean vigorous action in self-defence and that vigorous action we feel we're justified in initiating by any means necessary.'

We chant Obama's 'Yes We Can', appearing to apply it to our own lives but forgetting that he was expressing awe at the way in which *the world had changed during Ann Nixon Cooper's 106 years. 'When the bombs fell on our harbour and tyranny threatened the world, she was there to witness a generation rise to greatness and a democracy was saved. Yes we can. She was there for the buses in Montgomery, the hoses in Birmingham, a bridge in Selma, and a preacher from Atlanta who told a people that 'We Shall Overcome'. Yes we can. A man touched down on the moon, a wall came down in Berlin, a world was connected by our own science and imagination. Yes we can.'*

We read Churchill's words, we feel moved, patriotic and inspired. *'...we shall defend our Island, whatever the cost may be, we shall fight on the beaches, we shall fight on the landing grounds, we shall fight in the fields and in the streets, we shall fight in the hills; we shall never surrender, and even if, which I do not for a moment believe, this Island or a large part of it were subjugated and starving, then our Empire beyond the seas, armed and guarded by the British Fleet, would carry on the struggle, until, in God's good time, the New World, with all its power and might, steps forth to the rescue and the liberation of the old.'*

And then, we forget to mean it and to live it. We rally for others, but not for ourselves, we shine for the less fortunate yet struggle through the darkness, we give all we have and keep nothing back.

Allow your voice to be loudest. Speak out and say: 'Today, we will dream. Today we will best our past selves. Today we will be content but not complacent, because tomorrow and forever more, we endeavour to be fulfilled, by any means necessary. Yes we can'! and then mean it.

PERSPECTIVE

∞

IT JUST TAKES ONE

There's a reason that London Underground tell us to 'mind the gap between the train and the platform'. For as long as I have been using the underground network in London, there have been intermittent announcements asking passengers to 'mind the gap'. I know that as you read this, you can hear the well-spoken taunt of the woman who was paid far too much to tell us how to use our common sense.

But, it seems she was not paid enough: one week, as I was making my way from the Central to the Northern Line at Bank station, I noticed a young woman making a mad rush for the ready-to-close-and-beeping-like-mad train doors. It was quite obvious that she had missed the train but nonetheless, she thought she would try her luck.

Her piercing scream as she fell in the gap was not only heard in 5 boroughs, but was a reminder to all on the Central Line platform that there was a reason London Underground have the announcements in the first place. I was shocked and confused. My initial reaction was to rush to the woman's aid, but I noticed that most commuters carried on as if it hadn't happened. Were they so used to those kinds of mistakes that they did not bat an eyelid regardless of the consequence? I looked toward the CCTV cameras expecting at any moment for there to be a rush of LU staff attending the scene. Nothing. Perhaps they were also used to the stupidity.

Don't worry, the woman was fine, nothing more than her pride was hurt. The situation did pose a question to me about who I am though. What stopped me from running to her aid? Why did I consider her running for the train to be a stupid act? Where was my compassion?

The woman on the tube could have been seriously hurt or even killed, but I did not move. I now recognise the fact that embarrassment and pride kept me from reaching out and doing what was right. Regardless of her 'why', I could have been a kind face in the heaving rush hour crowd. My choice could have changed the course of her life, or at least her hour. I was so busy judging her choice to put herself at risk, that I forgot she might have been in pain.

The incident stayed on my mind for years and, I would say, became one of the turning points that helped to shape who I chose to become. The lady had her own responsibility to take for her choices that afternoon and I had mine. I wanted to be defined by my actions, not my inaction. I wanted to ensure that I did the right thing no-matter the cost. I wanted to make decisions that saved lives, not admonished their choices. I wanted to be a better person. I wanted to be sure that by any means necessary, I was the best version of me.

APPLICATION

∞

LETTER TO A FRIEND

Dear You,

Even when you're having a tough time, it always feels a bit better if it's on your terms, doesn't it?

Fear needs you. You don't need fear. Be patient. Wait. When your sun finally shows up, make sure you're there to see it. Defeat the demons. Send the rain away.

There are probably moments where you can't even laugh without excruciating pain. Time will reveal those moments as being memories to hang on to. The laughter despite its weight, will help to buoy you when you have no strength to swim.

Keep your sunshine. Don't give it away. It may be hard to manage loved ones' hopes and expectations about who we should be, what we should be taking, drinking, eating, breathing, wearing, listening to. You will regain your strength.

You have a choice to make about what you're willing to do by any means necessary to move forward.

You've proven yourself capable. Avoid relapses and bask in the light, while you float.

Others will benefit by default and when you find your strength, you will again move toward your goals.

Love, always x

∞

EVERY PART OF YOU

I do my best thinking whilst crying.
The tears release something in me that enhance my perspective.
I feel more, as most do, but I also realise more,
understand more and consider more.

So, instead of berating my need to cry,
I appreciate and accept that without my tears,
I would not be who I am.

Every part of you matters as much as the next.
Use them to your advantage.

∞

INDEPENDENCE

There's something about the feeling of independence. Nothing can beat the pride of being responsible for yourself. I believe that there are few times in our lives when we are truly overwhelmed by it.

We experience the thrill of independence most days in some shape or form, but I think the true feeling only happens on very special occasions - those times are usually called 'firsts': the first time you tell your parents you are going out, as opposed to asking; receiving your first bank card through the post and placing it safely in your previously empty wallet (although broke, in that moment, you feel as if you could pay the national deficit); passing your driving test (there is no feeling quite like it); the list could go on.

On assessment, the times when I was giddy with independence, were the same times I was moving forward with my life in a positive way.

I have come to the conclusion that if I want to keep feeling great about the choices I make, I have to keep adding to my list of firsts.

The direct link between achieving your best and feeling your best isn't a secret, but I wanted to share this reminder with you.

Now go forth and add to your list of achievements!
Live life on a high!

JOURNAL

∞

REFLECTION

By any means necessary means seeing the goal as attainable no matter what. It relates to standing alone when everyone else is facing away from you and it refers to doing what you have to no matter the cost.

Seeing ourselves and being seen as people who are respected should form the cornerstone of the ULTIMATE greenhouse we're building. We must do what is required.

As you conclude this chapter, look at the following questions. Consider how they make you feel. Be really honest. Then, settle down to write your own letter to yourself. Use what you have learned to populate the blank page. Start your letter, 'Dear Me, I've been thinking about....'. Once you've said all you want to say to yourself, signoff, 'I love you. Me x'.

Reflection Questions:

Who can you trust?
Whose rules are you playing by?
Who can you trust to be patient with you?
Who can you trust to be everything they tell you they are?
Are you giving fear credibility?
Who should you trust?

∞

LETTER TO MYSELF

Dear Me,

10

AND REMEMBER

Some things are predictable. If you don't put in the work, you won't succeed.

I was just looking for some material that I had written months ago. I searched many of the places I thought I'd kept it. I couldn't find it. I'd written it as a result of a burst of inspiration so I wasn't sure I could rewrite it. I decided to look in one last notebook, although I was convinced it couldn't be in there. I flipped through pages of notes on various topics, non of which satisfied my search. I paused a second when I came across a page of numbers. Bill payments? Money owed to or by me? The page diverted my attention. I had come across my 'win' page.

Next to the names of my family members, friends, charities, colleagues and projects were amounts carved out next to the imaginary disposable £1,000,000 I had won. I had it all figured out. I would give £20,000 to 3 people, £10,000 to 9, £7,500 to 7 others, £5,000 to 14 and £2,500 to 3 people. The remaining £720,000 would be split between my mum (£100,000), my best friend (£100,000), my business (£240,000), me (£240,000) and charities close to my heart (£40,000). I recalled how I felt when I wrote the list. I was happy with hope and excitement even though dreaming about it was just a fun task. I checked whether there were any names I would omit or add, then I shut the book and focused on writing.

Rereading that list reminded me about the power of dreams and how they can motivate progress. It would have been easy for me to go and play a line of numbers for the lottery as a result of the find but I did not and do not want to become wealthy by chance. I want my riches to be the result of skill, dedication and hard work. I want my success to be of my own making.

Looking for the notes of something I remembered being spectacular from my past was distracting me from my goal. What I had written may have been good, but I would never become a millionaire by spending too long looking for my greatness behind me. I had to create new masterpieces.

Finding the win list was motivation for me because I am more than well-equipped to conjure up sparkly things from the experiences that make up my story.

Whilst the list appears to focus on money, my real dream is about helping and sharing any wealth I possess with those I love and with those who need what I am blessed enough to have. One day I'll spend some time looking through the hundreds of notebooks I have filled over the years to see what else I have written or dreamed about. But first, I'll put in the work.

∞

SMALL BUT MIGHTY

She didn't know he was behind her. As she watched the CCTV footage back, her blood turned to ice. She'd been so stupid to have left her walking stick at home.

From the doorway of the study, Martin watched his mum as she watched the screen. He was angry that she blamed herself. It had been the middle of the day, for goodness sake! How was she to know that she'd be mugged. Effing opportunists! This was going to be a long road. Well, it might be, if he could ever get Mary to leave the house again.

Martin remembered the time she'd been mistaken for his son. She was slight in stature and extremely lean. At 5'7'', she wasn't short but he had to admit that, from behind, telling her apart from an adolescent boy was hard. The robber must have seen her silver hair and feeble walk, yet still choose to wrestle her to the ground. It was unforgivable!

Mary glanced at her only boy, his brows were even more furrowed than usual. 'Come on, love. It's ok. They caught him, remember?!'

His face softened... on the outside. He smiled at the only woman who'd ever held his heart as he entered the small room. It took just two strides to reach her. He leant down from his towering 6 feet and kissed her soft cheek, 'Next time, we enter the lotto online!'.

Mary knew what Martin needed to hear. He said he didn't want her to be scared to leave the house but she knew that he would be most happy is she never had to leave again. Her only child was so dear to her but he often forgot that she was parent. Mary wasn't afraid of the robber. In fact, she would quite like to see him again. Had they not caught him, she would have been scouring the streets. In her day, even the robbers had respect.

Martins mum grew up in the time where fear was a luxury. Although times had changed, she didn't know how to be anything but confident. She knew her grown son thought she blamed herself being old and weak.

He was wrong. Mary's only regret what's not having a weapon to hand. Her walking stick would have done just fine. Her age did not define her. She was small but she was mighty.

∞

LETTER TO A FRIEND

Dear You,

You have to seek inspiration in everything and refrain from just waiting for it to appear.

The start of a new day, year, month or decade is something to be inspired by. New years resolutions are valid. We just have to validate them.

Take it slow and steady.

Everyone is their own kind of brilliant. People may not know they need your until they see it.

When building a foundation, you have to first dig deep. Remember, no light can be found where the foundation must lay, but the closer you want to be to the sun, the deeper that foundation must be.

Dig so deep. Don't be afraid of the dirt. The harder you work, the dirtier you will get but have so much to gain.

Then stop. The time for building foundations is over. Now form your structure and raise it toward the sky.

Aim for the sun. You can't miss.

Love, always x

∞

THE JOURNEY

Don't worry about the speculation of strangers
or of gossiping acquaintances.

Forget about those who 'know best'
and ignore oversharing pessimists.

When the fuss dies down and
they have found something new to discuss,
you'll still be fighting the fight.

Take things in your stride and
do not be concerned about what others
think, say or do.

You'll realise soon enough
that tears cried over an insensitive
comment or a broken confidence are
tears wasted indeed.

There's no time to waste.

∞

I LET GO

'I often find the enemy of my
creativity to be my happiness.
I feel most inspired when I am so
close to the precipice that my
sanity's demise is almost certain.

Today, I stand here empty of
words, of inspiration and of
sadness, trying to remember
what it felt like to long for
happier times, but failing
miserably, because well, who
desires what they already have?'

'I conquered my pain, paid for it
with my tears. The devil stood in
my way but I had nothing left to
give him, so I offered him my
sorrow which he hungrily
devoured, believing we would
share my torment.

When he took hold, I let go.

My pain was now his to keep.
Behind his back, I found the
rainbow I was looking for. The
pain had gone. Entangled with
my genius, it became invisible
and I had to find a new way to be amazing.'

Recognise what is destroying you, then let it go.

I wrote I Let Go in one sitting. That isn't unusual. I am used to putting down my thoughts as I have them. The marked difference this time is the length of time it took me to conclude.

I started writing with a weight on my heart and by the end, I had found my sunshine and had decided to let go of what was hurting my heart.

The sun for me on this occasion was the act of writing. It allowed me to refresh my soul and to deposit all of the feelings that were restricting my growth onto a blank page where they could be seen and dealt with.

I didn't intend to be healed by the act, but I knew I wanted to feel better than I had been and I sought to find the thing that would enable that for me. I was lead by my heart, not by others' opinions about what I needed or why I should not have taken things to heart. I was moved towards healing by knowing myself and understanding what it would take for me to feel better in the long run.

The journey I have been on is never-ending and treacherous but bit by bit, I can see the healing taking place and that healing deserves my protection, so what does not serve me has to go.

You too can benefit from making space for and protecting your healing. Put safeguards in place, then strengthen them, often! You can't afford to lose.

∞

REFLECTION

When you don't know what to do or how to help, there is no harm in asking the questions: What do you need? How can I help? Those questions can also be directed inward. When you falter, what is it you need and who can help?

To actively work on creating the most effective ULTIMATE greenhouse, you need tools. Without them, your limitations limit your progress. There are work-arounds. You can use a spoon instead of a shovel or a pipette instead of a watering can but the results are affected and you end up wasting valuable growth time. Assess what you need and then find the right tools.

As you conclude this chapter, look at the following questions. Consider how they make you feel. Be really honest. Then, settle down to write your own letter to yourself. Use what you have learned to populate the blank page. Start your letter, 'Dear Me, I've been thinking about....'. Once you've said all you want to say to yourself, signoff, 'I love you. Me x'.

Reflection Questions:

Why are you holding on to?
What's your motivation?
Is it worth it?
What is it worth?
Can you afford to lose in some areas in order to win in others?
What would you be losing?
What would you gain by committing to playing the long game?
Who are you accountable to?

∞

LETTER TO MYSELF

Dear Me,

11

ALWAYS

...have an unfailing faith in yourself.

...believe the hope of children.

...celebrate your remarkable resilience.

...give your thoughts and feelings the respect they deserve.

...desire to do and be better.

...be fair and strive for fairness.

...remember to give yourself a break.

...acknowledge your greatness! You're human!

APPLICATION

∞

LETTER TO A FRIEND

Dear You,

I get it.

The feelings, the smells, the butterflies that aren't quite there yet, but they're close. You want to be here. You want to be present. You feel like you're doing something you've never done before. You're excited but you want to play it cool.

You love life in this moment. The experiences. They help and every time after that, you want to try to recreate the same feelings, the atmosphere.

This is growth. Embrace it. It is good.

Love, always x

∞

WEAR YOUR ARMOUR

At first, you'll have to fight a battle every day
not to go back to the darkness that engulfed you.
Understanding yourself is one of the biggest challenges
in being able to ascertain whether you were the darkness
or whether the darkness surrounded you so very completely
that you just couldn't see the you that existed.

Be aware of where that line is so that
you can start a renewal of the soul.
Consider your flaws, not from anyone else's
perspective but your own.
Decide what you are ok with keeping and let the rest go.

For your armour to do the job it was created to do,
you have to know when to wear it.

∞

IRREPLACEABLE

By learning who you are and placing a value on yourself, you become irreplaceable. That may not translate to being irreplaceable to the people you need to feel wanted by. Desire is rarely straight forward. Those surrounding us are unlikely to simply want or not want you. Instead, they may want the parts of you that suit them in an attempt to distract from the fact that they are working on or avoiding their own darkness.

Making yourself irreplaceable equates to knowing that you are worthy beyond measure whether others can see it or not. Valuing yourself may hurt at times. It can be lonely on the step we occupy because everyone is so focused on placing themselves where they belong they don't have time to share your step with you. You then feel tempted to step down and place yourself in a position better accessible by those you want to love you because you have attached your happiness to their desires.

True irreplaceability is patient and is willing to wait for those who are capable of loving the way we deserve. It is linked to identity, purpose and destiny which becomes legacy if we allow it to mature. This form of self respect knows that those attributes may not follow us if we lower ourselves for others' gain.

Awareness of our value allows for growth because we have unfettered access to the sun which makes us more attractive and in the end, this form of love for ourselves, attracts those who are lost in the forest trying to find their way. If you keep moving, they cannot lock onto your position, they can only glimpse you as you move.

Being irreplaceable means being irreplaceable to yourself first! Without ego, arrogance or pride, it means understanding that you have the power to warm others long after your sun has set in their lives. Let them choose you.

Show them how by choosing yourself.

JOURNAL

∞

REFLECTION

This journey is about you. Your growth, journey, faith, feelings and existence. It is an opportunity to grab the clay that shapes your life and mould it into whatever you need.

The best use of your clay would be to create a receptacle. One that can hold the earth, seeds, water and will help to promote growth. The clay alone won't do much but with all of the tools you're gathering, it will give you a sure foothold.

Your ULTIMATE greenhouse is nearly complete. The sun is great, the windows, the air, shelves, door and tables are in place, but in order for growth to be sustained, you need water. You must always combine the knowledge of where you have come from with a laser-like view of where you are headed. Only then can the sun and water work their magic in tandem. Reflection and direction evenly spread over the complete square footage of your life can only improve your outlook.

As you conclude this chapter, look at the following questions. Consider how they make you feel. Be really honest. Then, settle down to write your own letter to yourself. Use what you have learned to populate the blank page. Start your letter, 'Dear Me, I've been thinking about....'. Once you've said all you want to say to yourself, signoff, 'I love you. Me x'.

Reflection Questions:

What is the composition of your clay?
What will you make out of it?
How will it serve you?
Does your sun warm others?
How do you show it?
How much is your support worth to someone in need?
What does helping others do for you?

What is your armour made up of?
Do you protect and polish it?
How do you ensure that you're irreplaceable?

∞

LETTER TO MYSELF

Dear Me,

12

STAY SUNNY

Not so long ago, I remember spending a day just sobbing my heart out. It's not something I can really explain. I wasn't sad. Nor was I overly happy. I was just feeling everything so deeply. I saw the picture of a man saved from suicide because his community would not let him go and my heart was overwhelmed. It became full from witnessing the goodness of others and yet, it rattled from emptiness as a result of the Manchester bombing and every other daily atrocity humanity faces. I discovered a young YouTuber and listened to her story of loss. A widow at 26, I shed tears for her and prayed for her peace. I was again in touch with my affinity for understanding another's pain.

There are millions in pain. You're probably one of them. Whatever your trial, whether you feel able to reach out or not, please know that on that night and every night, my prayers are for you.

I am often reminded that sometimes you're not being warmed by the sun at all. On occasion, a reflection in the mirror is making you feel warm but it won't last because when the reflection dies, so will your warmth. When the real sun warms you, it lasts even during the night. You radiate warmth until the sun shines again.

Today, I realise that no matter how strong we think we are, we are not immune to an attack on our confidence. When that attack occurs, we can either fall cr rise. We may start to crumble and think that we are falling, but often, in order to rise, we must descend a little. Embrace your bad times and accept your failures. However, remember to appreciate your attributes for they are what you have to look forward to when coming out of the darkness into the light.

It's ok to be down. Your down times can serve you. Just remember that the sun means life so aim to stay sunny.

∞

SUMMER'S HERE

27 Luddick Lane. 2 large pepperoni pizzas, a portion of cheesy wedges, 2 tubs of nutty-choc ice cream and a 1 litre bottle of lemonade.

12 Green Edge. 1 personal margarita and some chicken wings.

124 Jersey Place. Meal for 6 - 1 large stuff crust veggie feasts/2 large Italian meat feasts. 1 x Nachos. 1 x Jalapeño Poppers and 3 x 1 litre bottles of cola.

Noah had been zipping around from delivery to delivery making people happy. It was nice turning up at front doors where people were expecting you and welcomed what you were offering. Of course, there were the few that were still unprepared, despite having made the order themselves 40 minutes before. They would welcome him then make him wait as they went to grab a purse, wallet or bag.

Noah was fine with the wait. He was a people-watcher and enjoyed imagining the before and afters of the people whose homes he only ever saw from the front door arch.

He had arrived at Luddick Lane with his recipients' life story perfectly planned. Two of the same large pizzas, ice cream and soda. There were definitely children in this house.

He was surprised to see a lone middle aged man waft to the door. At least, he looked like he wafted, so as Noah waited for the man to take the food from him, he held his breath and prayed that the guy would hurry. There was no light in the house except the porch lamp and that had only been turned on when he had rung the door bell. Maybe he was wrong. No children lived here.

At 8:30 on a Saturday night, he could usually hear one of the talent shows but this house was silent. Only darkness and smells that longed to escape lived here. The days were long and hot but no windows had been cracked in this property. That was clear enough.

Noah was glad to get away. Jersey Place wasn't far from Luddick so he quickly made his way the two minutes north to deliver the feast that would fill the bellies of those in the luxury apartments. Noah had been warned by his manager not to go into apartment blocks no matter how much the resident begged. He was to ring the buzzer and wait for the orderer to make his way to the main door.

He hated this part. They always begged him to bring the delivery to the door. He had heard all of the excuses: a mother whose sleeping child could not be woken nor left alone; a disabled man whose wheel chair had been nicked, and then he'd had the plain old chancers: 'Go on. You may as well.' The chancers offered a tip for the extra distance but Noah had learned that the £1.50 tip did nothing to cover the parking fine that he would receive for parking in the yellow zone.

He buzzed 124. No answer. He didn't need to guess what was going on in this house. Noah had brought them food many times. They were students. Rich students by the look of things but students for sure. He buzzed again and took his phone out ready to dial the number that had ordered. 'Pizza's here!' He heard a young man call back into the property. 'Someone will be down.' and the static disappeared.

Noah started to worry. He had been at smelly's house for 4 minutes, here for 7, so far and he still had another package to drop off. If it was too cold for the customers liking, he'd have to pay for it. This job was costing him more than he was making.

A moment later the inner door swung open and a young guy in a university hoody and expensive chinos made his way toward the main door. He pressed the release and strode past Noah almost unaware that he was there. Noah thought he'd recognised him as the person who paid the last time and his gaze followed the guy who was dressed far too warmly for the 32 degree evening. He must have been wrong. Hoody turned the corner and did not return. Noah spun to buzz again and was faced with an attractive girl who could have been no older than 24. He wasn't sure why he had fixated on her age. She had car keys and a wallet in her hands and was reaching toward him for the boxes. 24. She was divine and she must be 24.

'Hey, how much do we owe you?' her voice even sounded like she was 24. '24', Noah said before shaking himself out of the creepy trance he had found himself in. 'I mean, £42. It's the meal deal.'

She smiled and paid him what she owed.

He stood waiting for her to disappear through the inner door before he answered the phone that had been vibrating in his pocket for the last 30 seconds. 'Boss, I'm on my way. You know how Jersey Place can be.'.

He rushed to his final delivery of the night. 12 Green Edge. The house was full of people. He hadn't expected that. When he arrived at the open door, he understood the personal pizza and wings. They had all sorts of take out food in the kitchen, which was directly in front of the open door. What he had assumed was a meal for a very lonely one, was in fact a meal for one with loads of company. He found the customer, handed over the goods and was gone.

It was past 9 now and Noah was looking forward to clocking off. He went straight back to the shop and started to take off his gear. Helmet, gloves, jacket. He placed them on the peg where they lived and sat on the bench below to change into his personal footwear.

'Not so quick, Noa.'.
'...you've gotta be kiddin' me, boss!?'
'I'm not but don't worry, you can deliver this one on your way home.'

Noah changed and washed his hands. He collected his car keys from under the counter and replaced them with the moped key.

He picked up the last minute drop off and made his way out of the building saying his goodbyes as he went.

As he'd not been expecting to go out, he hadn't performed his usual routine. It was only now that he looked down at the address he was to deliver to. 120 Jersey Place.

He was officially off duty so Noah decided to park properly and make his way to the front entrance on foot. He rang the buzzer and was surprised it was answered after a very short moment. 'Hey,' a voice crackled over the intercom. 'Hi, it's your food.', he rushed back, fearing they would leave him standing outside for a longer period than earlier that evening. There was a short pause before the soft voice transmitted again, 'Can you come up?'.
'I'm afraid company policy...'

It was pointless speaking. The customer had taken their finger off the button that allowed him to talk and had released the door. What the heck. It was the last drop off of the night and he wasn't in any danger of getting a parking ticket. He'd do it, just this once. The last thing he wanted to have to do was to go back to Speedy Pizza because the customer had complained that the food had arrived cold.

As he got out of the elevator on the 5th floor, he could hear the party fun coming from 124. He was grateful that 120 was in the opposite direction.

He turned left and made his way to the door. Noah gave a gentle tap on the solid wood. Two steps, a handle turned and then he was face to face with, '24'. She looked at him, puzzled. '24?'.

He was embarrassed. He was acting like a love struck teenager instead of the 24 year old that he was. He knew better. The girl took the food from his out-stretched hand and he thought he might have fallen in love.

'Thanks for coming up. My name's Summer.'

The evening was hot, Noah sweated from his brow. Life was good and Summer was here.

∞

LETTER TO A FRIEND

Dear You,

The story goes: there was once a beach so full of starfish that there was hardly any space to walk. Just along the water's edge was a little girl painstakingly throwing the starfish back into the sea one by one. A passing traveller saw the girl and asked what she was doing. She told him that she was returning the starfish to their home.

The sand was almost completely covered and the man was bewildered. Wanting to save the girl her pointless efforts, he told her that she could not possibly make a difference.

The girl flashed an almost undetectable smile as she gently returned another starfish to the sea. 'I made a difference to that one.'.

What we do is important, no matter how minute others believe the action to be. Keep making moves to improve the world that is within your reach. Before you know it, you'll have cleared the beach and the difference you made will be unmistakable.

Stay sunny. There is always someone who can be touched by your very existence. Hold on. Don't give up.

Smile through it and when the smile slips, look to others to cast light where the shadows fall.

Love, always x

∞

WERE YOU ENOUGH?

One day during the dusk of your life,
you may reflect on whether you gave enough,
lived enough and loved enough.

The most revealing question though,
will always consider whether you were enough.

How you answer will frame the rest of your existence.

What could you have done?
Will you look back with contentment?

∞

SEEK THE LIGHT

Finding the sun can be difficult, especially if you don't know where to look for it, but I hope that some of my experiences and insights will support you to identify tools that enable you to sit up and seek the light.

If nothing else, take this to heart:

Muddy water can't stop you. One person can make a difference.
Your choices define you. You are worthy of so much.

Get comfortable but keep going. Continue to seek the light.
You've got this.

Depend on the suns strength. When it's darkest, look up.
Your sunrise is coming. There's always hope behind the clouds.

Someone loves you. Let go of the lies that bind you.
Be courageous and selfish with your love.
Be prepared for your summer.

Know that you are enough - then do more to be even more.
Aim for the sky, keep the sun within your sights. Engage every part of you in your story.

Your journey matters. Strengthen your circle.
The clouds will part, the dawn will break, your dreams will be realised.

Battle on.
Your tenacity is remarkable. Pay it forward.
Appreciate the sun on your face.

Evolve into the phenomenal being you are destined to be.
You are mighty and irreplaceable.

You are valuable beyond measure. Live, love, be willing to change everything on the road to here, by any means necessary. And remember, always stay sunny.

JOURNAL

∞

REFLECTION

Getting to the end of an experience is always, always accompanied by a great deal or lack of emotion. Getting to the end of this chapter may fill you with a bit of both. Why? Because I am asking you to reflect on your positivity. We have to don our Polly Anna smiles until they are no longer associated with her but instead, reflect the person that we have become.

That may sound like permission to fake it but that's not quite accurate. Faking your smile until you make it is a tactic so pertinent to your success that you'd be foolish not to have it in your arsenal. What I am asking of you here, is to use everything you have learned about yourself thus far to create a sun-filled place in your heart that you can go back to when it's dark.

Most people picked this book up because they want to be told HOW to do that, but what I have learned over time is that your 'how' is personal to you. The sarcastic quip that ran off your friends' back may just cripple you - lack of sleep may not turn you into a zombie, but for others, it can change their whole week. You have to find what works for you and then decide whether it is well with your soul.

You have been designing your ULTIMATE greenhouse. It is working just as it is meant to. You have everything just as you want. But you mustn't forget your lock. Remember to protect your growth. That means no one else should be given easy access to your fruit. Hold the key and loan it sparingly. Taking risks and loving hard are ok, but putting your hand up to question a shaky narrative or waiting to pull into traffic until you're ready, are ok too.

As you conclude this chapter and the Sunny Days book, look at the following questions. Consider how they make you feel. Be really honest. Then, settle down to write a letter to yourself. Use what you have learned to populate the blank page. Start your letter, 'Dear Me, I've been thinking about....'. Once you've said all you want to say to yourself, signoff, 'I love you. Me x'. This is your last Letter to Myself. Make it a good one.

Reflection Questions:

Who are you now?
What do you want?
How will you get it?
What represents your sun?
How will you maintain it?
What difference will cultivating the light make in your life?

Now get out there and grow!

∞

LETTER TO MYSELF

Dear Me,

THE FUTURE'S BRIGHT

Give yourself a hand.
Your triumphs are yours
and even though you feel that they don't mean much
in the grand scheme of things,
I know what it took for you to get here.

I'm proud of you.
I hope one day, you can be proud of yourself.

EVALUATION

You got to the end. You should have 12 Letters to Myself now.

Take those letters and place each in a separate envelope. Remember which one is which. On the front of each envelope, I want you to put the following:

'Dear Me,
Open this when...'

You will know when the message you have written to yourself will be most valuable. Complete the sentence on each envelope, then seal them.

Keep your letters safe. You will need them.

You have concluded this book and have answered a range of questions that will start you on your journey to design and maintain your ultimate dream days.

The final questions on these pages are any day questions. You will need to come back to them on a regular basis to ensure that you are making the most of your life and protecting that life-sustaining sun.

Reflection Questions:

What adjectives describe you?
Which adjectives would you want to describe you?
What do you think about most often at the moment?
What is most important to you right now?
How can you prioritise what matters to you?
Who are you surrounded by?
What keeps you motivated?
Do you believe you can do what you set out to?
What would stop you from emptying your truck?
If we could see your world through your eyes, what would we see?
Are you ready to find and share your sun?

RESOURCES

Finding your sun may sound easy but it can be terribly hard. Below are some organisations who know how hard it can be and who have put tools in place to help support you through your sunless times.

Samaritans
Samaritans is a charity that offers support to people in emotional distress or for anyone who is struggling to cope.
116 123

ChildLine
Childline is a free, private and confidential service where children and young people can find support.
0800 1111

The Mix
Offers information and support on a range of subjects for under 25s in the UK.
0808 808 4994

Mind
Mind is a mental health charity, providing help for people with mental health problems.
0300 123 3393

Victim Support
Victim Support is an independent charity providing specialist emotional and practical support to victims of all crimes, whether or not the incident has been reported to the police.
0808 16 89 111

Citizens Advice
Citizens Advice provides free, confidential and independent advice to help people overcome their problems.
03454 04 05 06

Macmillan Cancer Support
Macmillan provides support to those affected by cancer.

0800 808 00 00

Sane

Sane provide emotional support and help to improve the lives of those with mental health problems.
0300 304 7000

Printed in Poland
by Amazon Fulfillment
Poland Sp. z o.o., Wrocław